Praise for THE HEART OF ENTREPRENEURSHIP

"Her toys took the market by storm, and in this book Melissa Bernstein shows what it takes to follow in her footsteps with your next big idea. She distills a career's worth of entrepreneurial successes into practical tips."

Adam Grant, PhD
New York Times bestselling author of *Think Again* and *Hidden Potential*, host of the podcast *Re:Thinking*

"Inspiring and generous, filled with insight and encouragement from someone who's done the work."

Seth Godin
New York Times and *Wall Street Journal* bestselling author of *This Is Marketing*

"An illuminating road map for creators, dreamers, and builders ready to bring their most authentic ideas to life. Melissa Bernstein expertly shares the recipe that helped her build a billion-dollar brand and guide hundreds of founders in turning a vision into a reality. I highly recommend reading this book if you need a dose of inspiration to start and scale your business."

Reid Hoffman
cofounder of LinkedIn, *New York Times* and *USA Today* bestselling coauthor of *Superagency*

"A nourishing blend of insight and action, *The Heart of Entrepreneurship* serves up a recipe for unlocking the creativity and entrepreneurial potential that lives within all of us. With Melissa Bernstein's inspiring stories and actionable guidance, you'll feel both fulfilled—and hungry to begin your own journey."

Jamie N. Jones, PhD
director for Duke Innovation &
Entrepreneurship and associate professor at
Fuqua School of Business, Duke University

"Melissa Bernstein's *The Heart of Entrepreneurship* is a rare and radiant offering. With the clarity of a seasoned founder and the vulnerability of a truth-teller, she invites readers not only to build businesses but to build lives of purpose, patience, and presence. Melissa understands that entrepreneurship is never just about external success—it's about the inner terrain we must navigate: fear, ego, shame, love. This book is a gift to anyone who feels the call to create and is brave enough to start from scratch."

Jerry Colonna
author of *Reboot* and *Reunion*

THE HEART OF ENTREPRENEURSHIP

THE HEART OF ENTREPRENEURSHIP

CRAFTING YOUR AUTHENTIC
RECIPE FOR SUCCESS

Melissa Bernstein

Cofounder, Melissa & Doug Toys

BOULDER, COLORADO

Sounds True
Boulder, CO

© 2025 Melissa Bernstein

Sounds True is a trademark of Sounds True Inc.

All rights reserved. No part of this book may be used or reproduced in any manner without written permission from the author(s) and publisher.

No AI Training: Without in any way limiting the author's and publisher's exclusive rights under copyright, any use of this publication to "train" generative artificial intelligence (AI) technologies to generate text is expressly prohibited. The author reserves all rights to license uses of this work for generative AI training and development of machine learning language models.

Published 2025

Cover and jacket design by Charli Barnes
Book design by Rachael Murray

Printed in the United States of America

BK07218

Cataloging-in-Publication data for this book is available from the Library of Congress.

ISBN: 9781649633897

eBook ISBN: 9781649633903

Doug, there's no one I'd rather have by my side on this entrepreneurial journey. Your unwavering support, wisdom, and partnership—both in business and in life—mean the world to me. You embody the heart of entrepreneurship, turning vision into reality with passion and perseverance. Thank you for believing in me and my ideas and for supporting me every step of the way.

CONTENTS

INTRODUCTION 1

part 1 **CRAFTING YOUR RECIPE**
Creating the Product or Service
Consumers Want and Need

1 **THE MINDSET OF AUTHENTIC ENTREPRENEURS**
A Start-from-Scratch Mentality 19

2 **GATHER YOUR INGREDIENTS**
Diving Deep into Your Area of Intrigue (AOI)
and Exploring Your Passions 49

3 **ALLOW YOUR INGREDIENTS TO SIMMER**
Taking Time to Spark Insight,
Inspiration, and Intuition 79

4 **YOUR RECIPE IS READY**
Unveiling the Solution to Your Problem 103

5 **ASSESS AND ALTER YOUR RECIPE**
Accessing and Allowing Feedback
to Refine Your Concept 121

part 2 **SERVING YOUR RECIPE**
Releasing Your Product or Service
into the World

6 **PRESENT YOUR RECIPE**
Connecting Your Product or Service
to Consumers   161

7 **FOOD FOR THOUGHT**
Tackling Entrepreneurs' Most
Pressing Concerns   195

DESSERT
The Icing on the Cake   231

RESOURCES   235

NOTES   237

ABOUT THE AUTHOR   243

INTRODUCTION

From as far back as I can remember, I've never been content with superficial answers. The surface-level, the obvious, the simple—they were never enough. Even as a young child, I often asked "why" so many times that adults would sigh in frustration, their patience worn thin. Likewise, my peers would roll their eyes, muttering that I needed to chill out. However, it wasn't about being uptight; it was about being curious. Rabidly curious!

I now realize that curiosity was the genesis of my entrepreneurial spirit, although I didn't have a name for it back then. At the time, I only knew that I had an insatiable desire to get to the core essence of whatever I was pursuing. Whether it was trying to understand how rainbows were created or dissecting the meaning of life, I wanted to truly know. I needed to unearth the deeper truths that most people seemed content with just skimming over.

One particular moment stands out vividly in my memory. I was seven years old in second grade, sitting with my classmates in the reading circle. My teacher was discussing current events and mentioned the phrase "supply and demand." Curious, I raised my hand and asked what she meant. She explained it as simply as she could, saying, "It's about how much of something there is and how much people want it."

This explanation was fine for the rest of the class, but not for me. I raised my hand again, pressing, "But why does that matter?"

My teacher responded, "Because it affects the price." But that explanation still wasn't satisfactory.

I continued, "But why does it affect the price?"

Now she was becoming exasperated. She said quite testily, "Because when more people want something than there is supply, they're willing to pay more to get it." But I still didn't totally understand.

I quickly followed up with "But why would they pay more?"

At this point, my teacher had had enough, abruptly concluding, "Because that's just the way it is." And although my curiosity was far from satiated, I had received the clear message not to ask any further questions.

I didn't realize it then, but that endless line of questioning wasn't about trying to understand supply and demand but was really about uncovering the nuances beneath the surface of a concept. I wanted to truly understand the motivations, the patterns, and the why behind the why. I was intent on learning how things worked, not just so I could replicate them but so I could reimagine them completely.

As I became an adult, I discovered that getting to the heart of things takes time. In fact, it involves much more than simply asking questions; it takes experiencing the answers firsthand. You can't just leap to the core truth; rather, you must engage in a deliberate process of navigating the many layers of frustration, failure, and painstaking progress before those deeper insights reveal themselves. I didn't accidentally stumble upon the heart of entrepreneurship; I earned it through curiosity, passion, patience, and the hard-won lessons life's challenges exposed. It was this relentless pursuit of truth and accessing the heart of the matter that not only delivered answers but, more importantly, unearthed a profound sense of purpose.

WE ALL HOLD THE INGREDIENTS IN OUR HEARTS TO INSPIRE CREATIVITY

If you had asked me to identify the heart of entrepreneurship and its essential ingredients at age twenty-two, when Doug and I founded our toy company Melissa & Doug (M&D), I would have stared at you blankly. Back then, there was no time to assess. We were in a fight for survival, trying to surmount continual hurdles and transform our vision into reality. It wasn't until many years later, after combining my three-decade experience with insights gained from mentoring hundreds of other entrepreneurs, that I began to understand which ingredients comprised the unique recipe for entrepreneurial success.

My call to mentor others came after finally lifting my head after twenty years of building M&D in fight-or-flight mode. I felt a powerful stirring to share those hard-fought lessons with other entrepreneurs, as they had become so firmly engrained and critical to our success that I was certain others could benefit from them as well. Our thirty-five years of entrepreneurship had been excruciatingly difficult, largely because we received minimal coaching, and most of the guidance we did receive was unhelpful and often downright misleading. For decades, we operated in the dark, repeatedly making the same mistakes. We knew that with the benefit of wise counsel from astute mentors, we could have saved ourselves considerable time, money, frustration, and emotional stress.

Moreover, connecting with like-minded peers navigating similar issues would have shown us that our challenges were common among all entrepreneurs, making our journey much less overwhelming and isolating. I began responding to the many unsolicited emails I received asking for mentorship. There appeared to be a shortage of mentors who 1) had navigated the entire entrepreneurial journey from idea to building out a full-fledged brand, 2) had distilled their hard-fought insights into concrete lessons for effective mentoring, and 3) were willing to voluntarily offer their support on an ongoing basis. I delighted in honing my coaching skills through speaking with entrepreneurs of all ages, across diverse business disciplines, and from varied backgrounds.

One of the most fascinating aspects of these mentoring conversations was that many became discussions on the search for life's meaning, finding one's unique gift, building self-esteem, overcoming fears, and facing so many difficult yet inescapable aspects of being human. I reveled in connecting with founders on such a deep, vulnerable level. I also felt particularly qualified to support them emotionally and cognitively, as I had confronted and learned to effectively navigate the very issues they were currently encountering.

In 2013, Doug and I created an accelerator program at Duke University called Melissa & Doug Entrepreneurs. This program empowers student founders to tap into their hearts, connect with their passions, solve meaningful problems, and address unmet needs. It also equips them to confront the inevitable obstacles they will encounter, become adept at overcoming those challenges, and engage in the process of bringing their ideas to market. Mentoring student entrepreneurs was incredibly fulfilling, as I was helping them give birth to and transform their heartfelt visions into unique gifts to serve humanity.

When I began mentoring, I had no clearly developed intuition of which ingredients comprised the recipe for success. Naively, I believed that every creator had an equal chance of bringing their ideas to fruition. In fact, I initially selected students for our M&D Entrepreneurs program who lacked the necessary skills to complete it. I was drawn to dreamers with remarkable imaginations capable of generating ambitious ideas. However, many struggled to narrow their focus, commit to one idea, and invest the necessary effort to transform it into a successful venture. They remained trapped in their thoughts, unable to take meaningful action instead of being driven by a heartfelt mission that motivated them to overcome obstacles and persevere to bring their innovations to life.

Conversely, I chose others who could home in on one idea but became easily distracted by extrinsic motivations and the pursuit of immediate growth. They focused exclusively on building a successful venture as rapidly as possible, aiming for high valuations and lucrative exits. As a result, their businesses lost all connection to their hearts and true motivations, becoming uninspired, contrived, and derivative. These ventures often failed to stand the test of time since, without a genuine heart connection, the founders lacked the love for their work, the patience, and the commitment to make a meaningful impact—qualities that truly define entrepreneurship.

After mentoring a large and diverse group of entrepreneurs over fifteen years, I started consistently observing similar traits and skills in those who achieved success. I began to intuitively grasp

- whether someone's venture was likely to succeed.

- what differentiated those who turned their creative ideas into viable businesses from those who didn't.

- what allowed certain ideas to resonate with consumers more deeply than others.

I became fascinated with discovering why some individuals continuously generated creative ideas that achieved market fit, whereas others became one-hit wonders, devoid of inspiration after their single success. Then there were those who spent their entire adult lives strictly following conventional paths, never once daring to conceive anything even remotely innovative. I came to understand that individuals driven by passion, patience, and purpose were far more likely to live creative lives and achieve lasting success. *Passion* fueled their desire to explore and pursue innovative concepts wholeheartedly, while *patience* enabled them to endure challenges and setbacks, dedicating the time and effort needed to fully immerse themselves in their chosen field. Then, deeply engaging with their craft and absorbing every lesson sparked groundbreaking ideas and cultivated a profound sense of *purpose* and direction in their creative ventures. Empowered by this purpose, they were driven to overcome challenges and became inspired to share their work with the world, ensuring that their innovations made a meaningful impact and resonated with others.

I knew that we were all born with boundless creative potential and the capacity to innovate, yet few of us seemed able to maintain that childlike openness essential for sustaining the passion, patience, and purpose needed for inspired creation as we matured. Many of those I mentored expressed dejection, often saying things like "I guess I'm just not creative" or "I wish I could be an idea person like you, Melissa!" This made me ponder: how can individuals rekindle their creative potential and reignite that sense of wonder? After all, they once possessed that childlike sense of awe. What was blocking their ability to return to their hearts and create freely?

To answer these questions, I set off on a journey to research creativity and analyze my own creative process. I reflected: Why had I created over five thousand unique products at M&D over a thirty-five-year span? How was I then able to seamlessly transition into a new category at Lifelines, inventing seventy-five new products with twenty-two patents pending? Most intriguingly, why had I never faced a creative block in my career? What unique recipe was I following that made this possible?

I realized that the heart of entrepreneurship—and the ability to cultivate the passion, patience, and purpose needed to generate extraordinary insights and groundbreaking concepts—lies in a deliberate and structured process, much like following a recipe. The encouraging news is that this process is accessible to anyone willing to embrace possibility, uncover their own flashes of brilliance, and invest the necessary time.

Creativity flourishes in an environment of complete freedom, where a blank canvas ignites the imagination. That reservoir of creativity is deep within every one of us and can be tapped into again and again! In the pages ahead, I will guide you through the process of rediscovering and harnessing your creative potential, aligning it with your heart's desires, and reigniting the passion and purpose that fuel your journey.

TWO OBSTACLES TO CREATIVITY AND AN ENTREPRENEURIAL MINDSET

The passion, patience, and purpose essential to sparking creativity aren't exclusive qualities; they're accessible to everyone. However, as we age, we often become disconnected from those vital entrepreneurial ingredients that naturally reside in our hearts. This disconnection dulls our sense of purpose, making it challenging to tap into the passion and patience that fuel innovation and inspire original ideas.

The primary obstacle to creativity is fear, a natural response to a clear and present danger that is often shaped by past experiences, including failures. Closely related is anxiety, which arises from our struggle to tolerate the uncertainty of potential future threats or challenges. As existential philosopher Alfried Längle notes, "Anxiety is the price we pay for freedom and creativity. There is no existence without anxiety. Our existence is fundamentally insecure." This reminds us that fear and anxiety are intrinsic to the human experience and cannot be avoided.[1]

Dr. Emmy van Deurzen expands on this, explaining that "anxiety arises in the gap between certainty and possibility. Entrepreneurial thinking, by definition, must navigate both potential and the unknown, creating a fertile ground for anxiety. To foster creativity and discover the true heart of entrepreneurship, one must learn to endure this discomfort." She emphasizes, "You can only be creative if you allow for possibility . . . and you will need to learn how to bear with anxiety if you want to be creative."[2]

To think more entrepreneurially, you must discover how to accept, manage, and even harness fear and anxiety. This requires overcoming the challenging aspects of being human and having an unhealthy ego. An unhealthy ego feeds off distorted self-perceptions and behaviors that disrupt personal growth, relationships, and overall happiness, including defensiveness, arrogance, control issues, insecurity, shifting blame, and rigidity. In contrast, a healthy ego has a balanced and realistic sense of self-worth and confidence.

Many of us remain trapped in that unhealthy, ego-driven reactivity, preventing us from engaging our responsive hearts. True creativity only emerges when we untether ourselves from certainty, embrace the terror of the unknown, and allow possibilities to unfold. By doing so, we catalyze our full potential and allow new ways of thinking and groundbreaking ideas to put down roots and flourish.

When you step into the unknown and bring forth ideas from that blank canvas of imagination, it's natural to feel anxious about whether those concepts will be considered "good enough" or whether they'll face criticism and rejection. Since humans are biologically wired to connect, find social acceptance, and belong, this overwhelming sense of anxiety may prevent you from exposing your ideas to others for fear that they might not measure up to expectations. Our self-esteem is closely tied to how others perceive us, and receiving negative feedback about your ideas can make you feel judged and engender deep feelings of unworthiness and insecurity.

Generally, people are also uncomfortable with conflict and tend to seek harmony rather than fight for their ideas when they are challenged. To untether from an unhealthy ego and connect more with your heart, start by recognizing the protective function of the ego. Engage in a daily practice of reframing its negative beliefs into more constructive and honest ones. I struggled significantly with my unhealthy ego and worked with a cognitive behavioral therapist for five years to identify damaging thought patterns. Over time, I learned to reframe these thoughts into supportive, realistic beliefs. I continue this practice daily and will do so for the rest of my life.

The secondary obstacle to reaching your creative potential is impatience driven by the urgency for quick success—often cited as the primary reason entrepreneurs fail to achieve market success. Entrepreneurs generally feel intense pressure to reach a destination, lock in on a concept, and take the quickest route from their initial idea to building out the product or service. Many develop a rush mentality with the need to "arrive" at a finished concept too quickly.

The term "arrival fallacy" was coined by Tal Ben-Shahar, who claimed that people who experience the arrival fallacy often start off unhappy and reach for a goal that is supposed to cure their sadness.[3] When they find that success doesn't fix their unhappiness, not only are they disappointed, but they may end up feeling hopeless and depressed. Often, the arrival fallacy only makes unhappiness and mental states worse. This is because once we "arrive," we may become disengaged since our lives are suddenly devoid of meaningful activities. Society has conditioned us to believe that happiness is contingent on achieving goals that prove us worthy and acceptable to others. Therefore, entrepreneurs often charge ahead before fully evaluating the merits of their idea, quickly enlisting designers, artists, engineers, factories, and employees and racing to get their concept to market before they even have a solid understanding of their industry and competition. However, research has shown that achieving specific milestones doesn't bring happiness, at least not on a long-term basis, as the anticipated happiness either is fleeting or doesn't meet expectations.[4]

This impulse to rush may also arise from entrepreneurs' desire to scale quickly and look appealing to potential investors. This haste can prevent them from dedicating the necessary time for true revelations or a unique idea to emerge, shortcutting the most critical (and what should also be the most enjoyable) parts of the process of gestation, due diligence, and evaluation, where they meticulously test and hone their idea.

When entrepreneurs rush the creative process, disallowing their idea to unfold naturally, failing to understand all aspects of their problem, or lacking a deep proficiency in their area, they often mistake a recycled idea that doesn't offer anything novel to society for an amazing one. Putting too much pressure on the outcome leads to faulty, unfinished, or me-too ideas that fail to resonate with a broad audience. Through my own experiences, I have learned that building anything of deep significance requires passion, patience, and deliberate effort. Slow and steady usually wins the race! The creative process cannot be rushed; great concepts necessitate years of learning, discovery, and refinement to fully mature.

Moreover, our fast-paced lives heighten the demand for instant gratification, making it increasingly difficult to embrace uncertainty and let the creative process unfold naturally. This undermines our ability to be patient and allow authentic ideas to emerge. As a result, we end up prioritizing speed over depth in our creative pursuits. The emphasis on quick wins and instant feedback can make delayed gratification feel threatening to our immediate comfort and satisfaction, further obstructing our ability to connect with the heart of entrepreneurship. Yet by slowing down, embracing the journey, and allowing the process to unfold organically, we create space for the true entrepreneurship recipe to emerge—one that will be revealed gradually through the steps, stories, and lessons in the pages ahead.

MY INSPIRATION IN CRAFTING THIS RECIPE

I have had the extraordinary experience of starting with just a simple mission and vision, ultimately building it into a multibillion-dollar brand with M&D. In 2024, after surpassing one billion toys sold, Doug and I sold M&D for $1 billion. Now we've joined forces once again to tackle the new category of well-being with our second company, Lifelines. I feel incredibly fortunate to currently have two consumer brands featured in major retailers like Target, Amazon, and Walmart simultaneously!

In 2021, I published *Lifelines*, my memoir about transforming deep loneliness and existential despair into radiant light through creating children's toys. The capacity to wrestle inner chaos into something tangible and impactful through harnessing creativity became my lifeline. I finally felt an authentic sense of purpose, realizing that if I could access meaning through tapping into creativity, then others could too.

During my book's media tour, I spoke to students from the Inner MBA in a session moderated by Tami Simon, founder of Sounds True, a multimedia publishing company that aims to support personal growth and spiritual awakening. Tami also co-founded the Inner MBA, a nine-month online certification program that helps business professionals develop their inner skills and grow their careers. By then, I had been on a grueling road show with multiple engagements each day, and the repetitive nature of answering similar questions had begun to feel formulaic, leaving me simply "going through the motions."

However, the moment I began speaking with Tami, I was struck by a profound and unique emotional experience. I felt deeply moved on a soul level by Tami's provocative questions and the intense engagement from the Inner MBA students, which created a palpable sense of connection. After the session, my only reaction was "What just happened here?" That experience made me know, with every fiber of my being, that I needed to continue my association with that inspired program.

My sense of connection was further validated when I received over fifty emails the following day from the Inner MBA students requesting personal mentorship, highlighting the significant need for guidance within the program. Despite having a full-time role building our new company, Lifelines, I felt compelled to pursue this alliance further. In an uncharacteristic and bold move, I approached Tami and, despite my terror, expressed my desire to take on a more formal role to support these remarkable founders.

For the following class of Inner MBA students, I became the program's first Entrepreneur in Residence, tasked with creating and delivering unique content for six interactive workshops. I never imagined I would have twelve full hours to engage with these students, which also meant determining what exactly to present during those sessions. I had never created that type of content before and had no idea where to start. In fact, I initially considered taking the easy way out by simply calling all six sessions "Ask Me Anything." That way, I could avoid preparing formal content and dedicate all 120 minutes to answering students' most pressing questions. However, I already knew that individuals were generally hesitant to share personal questions in front of strangers. Perhaps I could reserve the last forty-five minutes of each session for questions, but I still needed to provide seventy-five minutes of meaningful content during the first two-thirds of the sessions so everyone would feel comfortable enough to ease into the question-and-answer part of the session.

I did not anticipate this level of preparation when I asked to be part of the program. What had I gotten myself into? Yet, despite my apprehension, I knew I was capable of crafting and delivering a worthwhile series. Although developing the sessions was as labor-intensive as taking on another full-time job, it was immensely rewarding, allowing me to distill my most essential entrepreneurial lessons into a cohesive curriculum.

Following my curiosity led me on an extraordinary adventure. Driven by a transformative experience and the courage to explore its potential, I developed six original-content sessions for the Inner MBA program and participated in multiple live webinars with Tami Simon. Most importantly, as I shared my personal journey and lessons with the first cohort of students, I had a life-changing revelation: using my hard-earned entrepreneurial insights to help others navigate their journeys felt like my true calling. This epiphany marked the pinnacle of my mentorship experience, crystallizing fifteen years of knowledge into actionable lessons for entrepreneurs. Ultimately, these sessions became the book you're holding.

Entrepreneurship can be a terrifying, lonely endeavor for many. The 2024 Founder Resilience Report highlights a stark reality: "The fact that 93% of U.S. founders report signs of mental health strain, with stress and anxiety levels five times higher than the UK national average, should be a wake-up call for us all. Despite 92% of founders expressing passion for their work, only a small fraction feel adequately supported. Just 43% feel they have a strong support system, especially as their ventures grow, and 76% report feelings of loneliness."[5]

Entrepreneurs need guidance to turn their innovative ideas into reality. Drawing from my experience from mentoring hundreds of entrepreneurs and navigating the joys and challenges of building transformative businesses, I've made it my mission to share the recipe that has shaped my journey. These lessons are here to empower founders to overcome obstacles, unlock their potential, and bring their boldest visions to life.

SETTING THE TABLE

In the chapters ahead, you'll discover the recipe to unlocking your creative potential and cultivating the passion, patience, and purpose that define entrepreneurial success. This book is not just about starting a business; it's about uncovering the essence of what makes ideas resonate deeply, solving real problems, and creating something that truly matters. You'll learn how to rekindle your boundless curiosity and wonder and channel them into innovation, understand what differentiates successful ventures from those that falter, and explore how to overcome the barriers that stifle creativity and derail progress through developing strategies to embrace uncertainty and build resilience. You'll also become adept at following this recipe and utilizing its ingredients to craft a vision, refine your ideas, and engage in action to turn your aspirations into reality.

Most importantly, this book serves as a guide to help you rediscover your heart's deepest passions and align them with your creative pursuits. It's about embracing the messy yet magnificent process of creating and finding a powerful sense of meaning and fulfillment in the work you do. Join me on this journey of self-discovery, innovation, and impact as we unearth your full potential together!

HOW THIS RECIPE CAN ENRICH YOUR ENTREPRENEURIAL JOURNEY

Conceiving innovative products and services, solving problems, and thinking creatively are possible for everyone and follow a clear and straightforward process. To illustrate the steps of this transformative innovation formula, I'll use the metaphor of your brain as a bustling commercial kitchen churning out innovative recipes to satisfy discerning diners. In this context, the term "recipe" represents your ideas, concepts, products, and services. To guide you through this innovation recipe, I'll introduce five key elements:

- **STORY NUGGETS:** Personal anecdotes and lessons learned from mentoring entrepreneurs

- **A TASTE OF PRACTICE:** Practical activities to help you integrate these lessons into your daily life

- **A FULL SERVING OF PRACTICE:** A deep dive into one core practice to enhance your innovation process

- **CHEW ON THIS:** A hands-on exercise designed to help you apply the concepts independently

- **CHERRY ON TOP:** Key takeaways at the end of each chapter that summarize the most important insights

To create these delectable recipes, you must begin by gathering a wide variety of ingredients. In a restaurant, these ingredients are sourced from local specialty stores, supermarkets, and farm stands. In entrepreneurship, however, these ingredients come from a multitude of personal life experiences.

Whether inventing products, services, or novel recipes, you'll gather the freshest ingredients from your life experiences, store the general ones in your mind's pantry, combine the most intriguing ones in the right proportions in stockpots, allow them to simmer for as long as necessary, and taste them. You'll also have others taste your creation, assess it, and adjust it as needed. When it's ready, you'll serve it up to your hungry customers.

Throughout this methodical process, you may be plagued by fear and anxiety, worrying that your final creation may not be satisfying or well received by your diners. You may also feel a constant urge to churn out recipes at an overwhelming pace and deliver finished recipes faster than feels sustainable. However, despite these inevitable challenges, it's crucial to stay the course and allow the process to unfold organically. Only then will you create countless delicious and original recipes that delight the masses.

The heart of entrepreneurship is characterized by resilience and adaptability. The journey is rarely linear; setbacks and failures are part of the process. Those who succeed are often those who can learn from these experiences, pivot when necessary, and remain committed to their vision. Ultimately, discovering the heart of entrepreneurship means aligning one's goals with a greater purpose and being driven by the desire to create lasting change. It's this combination of passion, patience, and purpose that truly defines what it means to be an entrepreneur.

When individuals cling to their usual thought patterns and apply established rules, they rely on familiar knowledge and methods. This ensures that their ideas remain unchanged, limiting innovation and maintaining the status quo. By guiding your thinking through the process detailed in the chapters ahead, you can elevate any concept, product, or business into something genuinely authentic and profoundly meaningful, amplifying its ability to resonate with others and contribute to a greater collective purpose.

part 1

CRAFTING YOUR RECIPE

Creating the Product or Service Consumers Want and Need

1

THE MINDSET OF AUTHENTIC ENTREPRENEURS

A Start-from-Scratch Mentality

To conceive innovative recipes the world has never before tasted, it's essential to *start from scratch*, a mentality fueled by curiosity, exploration, discovery, and passion. "Start from Scratch" implies beginning your process or project without using any prior recipe or existing resources to build upon. In essence, it means emptying the pot of what was previously made and starting fresh, free of preplanned ideas of what you will create today. Adopting this mindset is a lifelong practice and takes overcoming the unhealthy ego's fear of not knowing or not having a rigid plan to follow. I know this terror intimately as a product creator who starts from scratch every single day. It's a daunting task because each night, the pages of my cookbook are wiped clean, and every morning, I must begin again with no existing recipe.

I have lived the adage of "You are only as good as your last product" for thirty-five straight years of product creation, feeling that my reputation—and worth—are riding solely on my most recent success. During my thirty-two years at M&D, I created over five thousand different products, starting from scratch each time and adopting the mindset needed to maximize the chances of birthing not only a novel product but one that "sold like hotcakes." And over decades, that attitude has become woven into my identity and my unwavering knowledge base.

Embracing a "Start-from-Scratch" mentality involves following a number of key principles. Five of the most essential are dropping all preconceptions and opening the mind to learning, cultivating curiosity, having the courage and confidence to engage in continual trial and error, learning how to shut out distractions and extraneous stimuli, and detaching from your unhealthy ego. I'll cover each of these principles for you in detail now.

DROPPING ALL PRECONCEPTIONS AND OPENING THE MIND TO LEARNING

A Start-from-Scratch attitude involves starting from a state of "unknowing" and seeing everything fresh, as if for the very first time. Zen monk Shunryū Suzuki wisely said, "In the beginner's mind there are many possibilities, but in the expert's there are few."[1] The beginner's mind spends as much time as possible in the present moment because *we can only conceive new ideas in the present moment*. Entering a state of unknowing takes achieving supreme awareness and involves practices that cultivate openness, mindfulness, and a readiness to move beyond preconceived notions. In essence, you must return to a playful, childlike state because it reflects the curiosity, wonder, and freshness that characterize transformative learning and discovery!

Story Nugget

> As someone whose anxiety is deeply intertwined with perfectionism, I find that the thought of my products determining the success of our company—and the livelihood of so many—can

be overwhelming. Over time, I've discovered my secret ingredient: the Start-from-Scratch mentality. This approach enables me to create again and again, turning what feels immobilizing into a continual cycle of renewal and possibility. Without it, I'd be paralyzed by fear—fear of the future, fear of how others might judge my work—and that fear would choke my ability to create freely and authentically.

The beauty of this approach lies in its simplicity. I don't have to force progress! It's not about doing anything; it's about being open—fully present, aware, and receptive. It's a practice of embracing everything as it comes, observing, exploring, and welcoming each moment without resistance. Like your stockpot, your mind must start with nothing in it so you can freely collect new ingredients and receive inspiration. When I remind myself that the answers are always there, waiting to be uncovered—like stones to turn over or lids to lift off simmering pots—the pressure eases. I can settle into the creative flow as ideas take shape organically, flowing from the openness and engagement in the process. Whenever anxiety begins to creep back in, I return to this mindset of starting fresh. By clearing my mind and looking at the world through new eyes, I remind myself that every moment is an opportunity to begin again.

A Taste of Practice

Your personal practice to open the mind to learning may include:

- **SPENDING TIME IMMERSED IN NATURE** and letting its interconnectedness be a reminder to accept life's natural flow and relinquish the need for control. Nature is my inspiration because it embodies beauty and transformation in its purest forms. Its boundless mystery and incredible force spark my curiosity and wonder, and its continual ebbs and flows and powerful metaphors evoke my full spectrum of emotions. Nature also offers a safe, non-judgmental space for calm, reflection, and rebirth, serving as an endless source of ideas and a reminder of life's interdependence. Nearly all my epiphanies arise while I'm walking outdoors.

- **CELEBRATING EFFORT VERSUS OUTCOME** and finding joy in the act of creating in the present moment. This means letting go of attachment to a finished product and the need for validation. Try to revel in the beauty of creating something from nothing, whether the product achieves extraordinary commercial success or not.

- **BECOMING AWARE OF YOUR BELIEFS, ASSUMPTIONS, AND THE TENDENCY TO JUMP TO CONCLUSIONS** by actively questioning, asking why, considering diverse alternatives, and being open to changing those rigid opinions and beliefs.

- **ENGAGING REGULARLY IN JOYFUL AND CONTEMPLATIVE ACTIVITIES** that keep you squarely in the present moment, such as listening to music, beachcombing, walking, reading, or journaling. This is where all creativity lies.

- **EMBRACING AND BREATHING INTO YOUR HUMAN NEED TO CONTROL THE UNCONTROLLABLE FEAR OF UNCERTAINTY** and becoming okay with letting the future unfold without needing to know exactly what will happen. After all, it is impossible to predict the future, and trying to do so only wastes valuable energy.

- **STEPPING OUT OF YOUR COMFORT ZONE,** trying new things, and exposing yourself to new experiences and perspectives that stimulate your curiosity and growth.

- **CONNECTING WITH EXPERIENCED TEACHERS AND SPIRITUAL GUIDES** who provide insight and wisdom and share lessons from their own journeys of self-discovery and awareness.

A Full Serving of Practice

I spent my early life fixated on the end goal, completely tethered to the outcomes of my pursuits. I believed that my worth was measured solely by my achievements and how well my products were received. I would get stuck in my head, constantly worrying: *What will others think of my idea? Will they like it or reject it?* This mindset made the creative process stressful and hindered my ability to be fully present. As I matured, I realized that I can only control what I create in this moment; I cannot dictate how others will react in the future. Worrying about the future just expended vital energy that could be channeled into creativity. To remind myself to keep returning to the present moment and funnel all my unsettledness into expression, I wrote the following mantra:

> Step on out of the head
> *Moving into the heart*
> Free to channel all dread
> *Into jubilant art*

Not surprisingly, the more I moved into my heart and created from passion and purpose, the more my work resonated with others. Today, I create entirely in the present moment, knowing my power comes from continually channeling and sharing my distinct perspective with the world. Sometimes my concepts will resonate, and sometimes they won't—but I don't sweat it either way, trusting that everything unfolds exactly how it's meant to!

Chew on This . . .

Try this **Mantra Recipe** exercise to help shift your focus from worry and rumination to inspired creation:

- **BEGIN BY ACKNOWLEDGING YOUR EXISTING STATE:** "I feel the fear but step away."

- **ARTICULATE YOUR INTENTION:** "Into the beauty of today."

- **AFFIRM AN ACTION STEP:** "And channel worry into art."

- **CONCLUDE WITH A POSITIVE NOTE:** "For this is where I need to start."

Once you've created your own mantra, set aside a few minutes each day to read it aloud or write it in your journal. Use it as a handy grounding tool whenever you find yourself becoming anxious about how your creations will be received or focusing too much on the future.

CULTIVATING CURIOSITY

Repeatedly asking "why," "how," and "what if" is the key to discovering new ways of doing things and new problems that need to be solved. Innovators possess an insatiable curiosity and enthusiasm to unearth revelations never accessed by humans and have a genuine interest in and passion for discovery. That means being entirely deliberate about opening yourself up to wonder. It starts with becoming supremely conscious, aware, and present to the extraordinary wonders that already exist around you. *Be as absorbent as a sponge, and take in everything you can from each and every experience.*

A simple way to practice this awareness is by tuning into your senses in whatever you are doing. What are you seeing in this very moment? What are you hearing? What are you smelling? Your senses anchor you in the present moment, and by focusing on them, you deepen your presence in your life. This presence is essential for creativity because creative ideas emerge when you leave no stone unturned and recognize that opportunities await wherever you look! In fact, in a 2014 study, a team led by Matthijs Baas revealed that to be creative, you need to be "trained in the ability to carefully observe, notice, or attend to phenomena that pass your mind's eye."[2] Don't take anything at face value; instead, find value in all experiences and things, no matter how seemingly trite. Believe that deliciously sweet chocolate chips are always nestled within the cookie dough. With a little patience, you'll uncover these rich surprises in every bite!

Step out of your comfort zone and make life unfamiliar by engaging in new and different experiences. Embrace "the verb of life"—the active pursuit of exploring, investigating, discovering, and fully participating in your life. Have the courage to follow your sparks of interest and passion, and be motivated by enthusiasm and intrigue for whatever you're doing—or stop doing it! Use your level of commitment and drive as your litmus test for your pursuits. A high level of genuine intensity is essential to build the fortitude needed to persevere through the challenges that will arise on your path.

Keep collecting more fresh experience ingredients every day to fuel innovation. For example, try a new hobby, explore a different area of your city, or engage in conversations with strangers of diverse ages and backgrounds. You'll need a continual abundance of experiences to conceive inventive ideas, and each fresh experience adds to your pantry of inspiration, helping you innovate and think creatively. If you engage in too much predictable routine, your habitual patterns will regurgitate the same old answers rather than novel insights.

Curiosity also values the process of engaging in life experience above a *rush mentality and attaining a rapid outcome*. It is connected to a more positive mindset and experiencing more enjoyment and less frustration. Adopting a curiosity approach naturally takes patience and the ability to accept unknowns because we are delaying the rush to resolution and allowing the process of collecting ingredients to unfold. This takes extreme confidence and the belief that novel insights take time to arise, leading to a more satisfying experience in the end. Rather than needing instant gratification and an immediate and certain outcome, curiosity promotes the willingness to wait and allow the chance for true understanding.

Story Nugget

Asking one simple question purely out of curiosity and seeking its answer led to the creation of our toy company, M&D. Doug and I naively wondered, "Where can we find the classic wooden toys that were the hallmark of our childhoods?" When we traveled to toy stores in search of that answer, we saw that the handful of wooden toys that did exist were dull, lackluster, and exorbitantly overpriced. This discovery illuminated a potential need in the market and became our three-decade problem to solve: can we create beautifully designed, high-quality wooden toys that are affordably priced? We became passionate about reinventing tired concepts and creating entirely new categories of innovative, accessible playthings—launchpads to spark fertile imaginations and help children discover themselves, their passions, and their purpose.

A Taste of Practice

Your personal practice to cultivate curiosity may include:

- **PURSUING** *whatever* **INTERESTS YOU!** Don't worry about where a topic or interest will ultimately lead, but simply follow the ones that genuinely spark your interest and let them take you wherever they wish to go. Start by selecting just one topic or area you've always wanted to learn more about, and schedule time to invest in it!

- **IMMERSING YOURSELF IN CONTENT** by reading books and articles, attending lectures, or listening to podcasts. Revel in learning, and actively seek to open yourself up to new ideas, topics, and ways of thinking whenever and however you can.

- **STRIVING TO BE A POLYMATH!** A polymath is someone who develops expertise or knowledge in multiple disciplines or fields of study. "Polymath" originates from Greek roots meaning "having learned much." Polymaths are characterized by their ability to gain proficiency across multiple disciplines with a depth of understanding that allows them to synthesize information from diverse sources to expertly address complex challenges and generate novel ideas and solutions.

- **CONTACTING EXPERTS IN YOUR AREAS OF INTEREST AND ACTIVELY SEEKING OUT OTHER STIMULATING MINDS** who are eager to engage in enlightening intellectual discussions and feed your mind with unique perspectives and viewpoints. In fact, these experts may disagree with your opinions and approaches and engage in heated debates with you that help you hone your ideas. Moreover, you may develop beautiful friendships with them. A few of my dearest friendships began when I reached out to these "strangers" to discuss my area of interest!

- **JOURNALING** to become a documenter of all things that surprise and delight you and reflecting on your experiences and observations to contemplate deeper meaning.

- **SHARING EXPERIENCES WITH OTHERS THAT FILL YOU WITH AWE AND WONDER** on a daily basis to demonstrate that beauty exists all around you. Perhaps your passions will even spark others' interest in them as well!

- **SAYING NO TO ACTIVITIES AND PEOPLE WHO DON'T LIFT YOU UP** and raise your vibrational frequency. You must cherish your time and protect it!

- **SCHEDULING SOLID BLOCKS OF TIME TO INVEST IN THE AREAS THAT FASCINATE YOU.** Commitment and perseverance are essential to pursuing your deepest interests and furthering your goals.

A Full Serving of Practice

There is so much content available these days that I can become obsessed with collecting as many enticing ingredients as I can. However, too much information ultimately clogs my brain, leaving little space for my own ideas to swirl and flow. Excessive content also triggers a sense of FOMO, making me anxious about never being able to ingest all the amazing material available in the world.

My practice to selectively choose and squeeze the most out of content includes 1) only listening to, watching, or reading things that genuinely interest me; 2) moving on to something else if it doesn't immediately captivate my attention; 3) actively listening and taking notes on what I am ingesting; and 4) slowly revisiting my notes while the episode is still fresh in my mind, allowing them to distill through my being and become new ingredients in my pantry. This way, the nuggets of insight become a permanent part of my repository of knowledge.

One of my friends often marvels at the way I can recall specific, salient details from the large amount of material I consume. It is simply through this active engagement and the process of revisiting the morsels that resonate most with me that I am able to extract their full value!

Chew on This . . .

Try this **Digest and Distill** exercise to actively engage with the content you consume and transform passive consumption into an active, creative process, extracting and retaining the most valuable insights:

- **LIMIT YOUR PORTIONS:** Select only *one* piece of content per day to consume—an article, video, podcast episode, lecture, or book chapter—that genuinely fascinates you.

- **CAPTURE THE FLAVOR:** After digesting the content, note a single standout concept or idea that deeply resonates with you. Avoid gorging yourself with too many takeaways.

- **ENHANCE THE FLAVOR:** Reflect on how your key takeaway connects to your initiatives, life, or current challenges. Write down one practical way you can apply or expand on this insight going forward.

- **LET IT MARINATE:** Take that most compelling nugget of wisdom and revisit it throughout the day, allowing it to blend naturally with your thoughts.

- **STORE IN YOUR PANTRY, ADD TO A RECIPE, OR SHARE:** At the end of each week, look over all your daily reflections and determine which ingredients should be stored in your pantry, which can be added to an existing recipe for depth and flavor, or which can be shared with a friend or colleague to further solidify it in your mind.

HAVING THE COURAGE AND CONFIDENCE TO ENGAGE IN CONTINUAL TRIAL AND ERROR

Entrepreneurs must embrace the truth that making mistakes and failing, then getting back up and trying again is the only way to learn and is essential for innovation. By developing the courage to look honestly at your failures for their critical life lessons, you will see that failure has an important function. It asks you whether you really want to continue persevering and perfecting your idea or if you would prefer calling it quits. It questions, "Do you love this venture enough to endure the fear of it failing?"

If you can mine your missteps for their wisdom, you can improve how you operate, hone your skills, and become increasingly proficient. Your failures are illuminating windows that show you where you went wrong, and studying them holds the key to your greatest insights. The lessons you learn from failing ultimately become your most valuable nuggets of wisdom—essential ingredients that fuel innovation, change, and growth.

Embracing failure takes adopting a mindset of positivity and believing that the more you fail, the more you succeed. I believe that negative experiences can be even more valuable than positive ones.

They help establish the guardrails for what doesn't resonate with you and what you won't tolerate in the future. This means you may need to test out many activities and have many experiences that you *don't find enjoyable* to find the ones that excite you. Try numerous pursuits as early as possible until you "fall in love with something," and retain this commitment throughout your life. Once you fall in love with something and develop a fervent passion for it, you will eagerly want to commit yourself to it. That devotion will be necessary to sustain your intense interest and effort for a prolonged period.

Story Nugget

Although there were numerous pretend-play shopping carts for children on the market, I wanted to create a steel version that resembled a full-sized supermarket shopping cart. The design process took nearly one year, and we were eager to find a manufacturer, knowing it would surely become one of our bestsellers. We shared our specifications with five different factories and requested price quotes. However, we were shocked when they all declined, stating that manufacturing a miniature steel cart was too challenging for them.

Despite our pleas, urging these factories to consider the shopping cart's potential as a bestseller, they remained unconvinced. My team suggested I abandon the idea, believing the cart was impossible to produce. Yet I refused to accept defeat. I traveled to China with my head of manufacturing, taking our prototype with us on the plane. After visiting nearly twenty toy factories, all of which turned us down, it dawned on us that a toy factory might not be the right fit. Finally realizing that we might have been looking in the wrong place, we shifted our focus to shopping cart manufacturers instead.

We eventually found a factory that produced carts for major US supermarkets. When we presented our design, they scoffed and said, "We make full-sized shopping carts, not children's versions." They started walking away, but we knew this was our last chance. Desperate, we ran after them, begging them to consider producing our cart and promising a substantial initial order—even though we hadn't yet sold any carts to customers. After nearly an hour of negotiation, they reluctantly agreed to manufacture our first order.

That pivotal moment occurred fifteen years ago. Today, our shopping cart remains one of our bestsellers, boasting ten thousand reviews and an average rating of 4.8 stars on Amazon. This journey taught us the power of perseverance and the importance of thinking outside the box to turn a dream into reality.

A Taste of Practice

Your personal practice to become more comfortable with trying and failing may include:

- **CHANGING TWO WORDS** to move from a victim mindset and believing that you are being treated unfairly to realizing that everything happens for a purpose and has valuable life lessons to teach you. Ask yourself, "*How* is this happening *for* me?" rather than "*Why* is this happening *to* me?" Every failure, no matter how terrible, has the capacity to teach you something valuable and help you grow if you can depersonalize it, examine it objectively, and extract its critical life lessons.

- **CONNECTING WITH OTHERS** and sharing experiences that help you see that *everyone* encounters failures. In fact, it's only through proudly displaying those imperfections and vulnerabilities that we become empathetic, relatable, and human. It's those scars, not a lack of them, that make us beautiful, strong, and resilient.

- **ACKNOWLEDGING THAT NOTHING GOES PERFECTLY** and setbacks are inevitable and expected along the entrepreneurial journey. In fact, once we realized that setbacks were inevitable, Doug and I began boldly embracing them, realizing that every challenge we surmounted only further separated us from our competitors.

- **LEARNING FROM THE EXPERIENCES OF SUCCESSFUL INDIVIDUALS WHO EXPERIENCED FAILURE** but persevered with their determination and resilience can provide valuable tips and build your confidence by showing that setbacks are part of the journey.

- **TREATING YOURSELF KINDLY WHEN YOU MAKE MISTAKES.** Try to give yourself the same level of kindness you would offer a good friend or a child who needed comfort after they tried their best but messed up anyway!

- **ABANDONING PERFECTIONISM AS YOUR GOAL.** Duke Professor Rachel Adcock earnestly stated, "There is no such thing as positive perfectionism."[3] That is because humans are naturally *im*perfect. If we strive to be perfect, we will always be disappointed in ourselves and avoid taking chances based on our fear of falling short. The more we can embrace our fallibilities and recognize that no one is flawless, the more we can relax and be kinder to ourselves.

- **BECOMING BETTER AT SEEKING CRITICISM, HEARING CRITICISM, AND ALLOWING OTHERS' FEEDBACK** to improve your recipes. Most people aren't trying to hurt your feelings with their comments but rather want to help refine your concepts! However, the unhealthy ego sometimes wants to take *all* the credit and disallow anyone else to share in the glory, even when their suggestions greatly enhance your original idea. Try to distance yourself from that ego and view criticism honestly and objectively to help you improve and grow.

- **TRYING NEW ACTIVITIES THAT PUSH YOU OUT OF YOUR COMFORT ZONE** and taking calculated risks that allow you to successfully prevail, develop confidence, and grow.

A Full Serving of Practice

It's easy to get stuck in a victim mindset, lamenting, "This isn't fair" and "Why me?" This perspective is disempowering because it makes you believe there's nothing you can do to change your circumstances. It also breeds negativity; if you think you cannot change your situation, you ultimately lose hope for the future. Of course, it's essential not to mask the truth and feign false positivity nor to suppress difficult emotions in an attempt to force optimism. Acknowledging reality—both its hardships and its lessons—allows us to process, adapt, and ultimately grow. And as I began to accept my full spectrum of emotions and take responsibility for creating meaning in my life, I realized I had the power to choose my attitude. I could adopt a mindset of negativity, convinced that everyone was out to get me and nothing would ever go my way—ensuring my own misery and spreading it to those around me. Alternatively, I could believe that everything that happened, even the seemingly terrible events and colossal failures, held lessons and silver linings. By looking at life through this more optimistic lens and believing there was unconditional meaning behind *all* experiences, I became much more likely to learn from my failures and bounce back from them! Today, whenever I find myself thinking, *Why is this happening to me?*, I remind myself of my love for bittersweet dark chocolate, with its complex blend of sharpness and sweetness. At first, its bitterness seemed too intense, but over time, I began to appreciate its depth, just as I've learned to find meaning and growth in life's difficulties.

Chew on This . . .

Try this exercise of **Squeezing the Best out of Life** to turn life's bitter moments into sweet ones bursting with growth and wisdom:

- **TASTE THE BITTERNESS:** When you find yourself stuck or facing a challenging situation, you may start thinking, "This isn't fair" or "Why me?" Catch yourself doing so, pause, and take a deep, long breath to ground yourself.

- **MIX IN CURIOSITY:** Replace your negative self-talk with the question "How is this happening for me?" Imagine the challenge as another ingredient in your life's recipe and an opportunity to add flavor and depth.

- **MAKE LEMONADE OUT OF LEMONS:** Identify one insight, lesson, or opportunity hidden in the situation or experience, no matter how small. Let it marinate in your mind.

- **SAVOR YOUR NEW BLEND:** Write down your reframed thought to help it stick. For example, "The unanticipated delay ended up giving me extra time to make product improvements." Reflect on how the reframing made you feel, and savor that feeling.

LEARNING HOW TO SHUT OUT DISTRACTIONS AND EXTRANEOUS STIMULI

Total immersion comes from embracing the present moment, letting go of the past, and not getting caught up in the future and what you intend to do or achieve. Supreme focus is the key to accomplishing anything of real significance. You'll need that level of attention to deeply immerse yourself in an area of interest and learn all you can about it. Those who can achieve a flow state are more likely to gain expertise in the areas that fascinate them.[4] However, there are a couple main obstacles that get in the way of supreme focus.

The first significant barrier is *judgment* and wasting vital energy criticizing and berating yourself or others for very human faults. Or *worry* in "crying over spilled milk" and wasting time dwelling on events in the past that cannot be changed. You cannot be receptive to inspiration when you're entirely consumed with admonishing yourself and others or lamenting past mistakes. In truth, this behavior squanders your vital life force and serves no meaningful purpose. Instead, funnel those precious resources into action—explore more, learn more, and create more!

The second key barrier to maintaining focus is the *pressure to secure an outcome*, which often leads to impatience and a rush mentality. Additionally, becoming consumed with petty matters can distract you from the areas that interest you most. To truly concentrate on a problem, you need to avoid becoming sidetracked by worries about your venture's future or what others are thinking of you or your venture. If you can reallocate the time and energy you spend worrying about the future and things beyond your control to the task you're doing right now, you will make far greater progress. The ability to return to the present moment and maintain peace of mind is essential to creating innovative work of the highest caliber.

Story Nugget

It's a common human tendency to get distracted by trivial matters as a way of avoiding business responsibilities that we find unenjoyable or challenging. One of those personally challenging activities for me is writing copy for our products. We've been designing sets of scented colored pencils for Lifelines, and part of my job is writing brief descriptions of each scent on their exterior. Each label needs to be unique, and I desperately want each of them to evoke a beautiful sense of nostalgia for the user.

Yet if I don't force myself to sit down and work diligently on them, I find myself gravitating toward everything *but* writing those descriptions since the task feels so overwhelming. It can take me as long as four hours to craft just twenty descriptions. This means I *must* hold myself accountable for tackling these challenging tasks by scheduling dedicated time to engage in the work and resist the urge to get up or do anything else until they are finished. When I create that focused space and hold myself accountable, I consistently make progress. But if I don't, procrastination takes hold, stifling my creativity and impeding me from achieving my goals.

A Taste of Practice

Your personal practice to become less overwhelmed and distracted may include:

- **BREAKING LARGE TASKS DOWN INTO SMALLER, MANAGEABLE STEPS** that make them less intimidating, shorter to complete, and easier to focus on.

- **LIMITING MULTITASKING,** which increases distractions and reduces efficiency. It's much more enjoyable and relaxing to devote your full energy and attention to each task, which also improves the quality of your work and productivity.

- **SCHEDULING CLEAR GOALS AND PRIORITIES EACH DAY** to help you stay focused on what needs to be accomplished and reduce the temptation to veer off track. Don't allow yourself to move on to the next task until you accomplish what you set out to do. I set multiple alarms on my phone each day to remind me to complete tasks that I would otherwise forget to do and allow to keep piling up. I complete the task the moment that alarm rings, avoiding the tendency to push snooze and postpone it to later. Doing so has been a game changer for me!

- **CREATING DISTRACTION-FREE, CALMING SPACES** and organizing your workspace to reduce clutter and visual distractions and help promote mental clarity.

- **REWARDING YOURSELF WITH STRATEGIC BREAKS** after engaging in a few hours of intense work. This not only gives you something to look forward to but helps rest and recharge your mind and body, which prevents burnout and improves your overall concentration when you begin working again. One of my daughters rewards herself with an episode of her favorite show after she completes a set number of pages of a challenging essay.

- **ENGAGING IN SENSORY ACTIVITIES** that help bring you back to the present moment whenever you find yourself getting caught up in unproductive activities. If you cannot seem to buckle down and get to work, get up and splash cold water on your face, play with your pet, listen to your favorite song, take a drive, go for a walk, or craft—to name a few of my favorite ways to ground myself before returning to work.

- **REFUSING TO LET COLLEAGUES, FAMILY MEMBERS, OR ROOMMATES INTERRUPT WORK TIME.** Since many of us now work from home, we may need to better communicate our need for focused and uninterrupted work time. This has been a challenge for me because my children assume that my presence at home means I'm always available to engage with them throughout the day. I feel terribly guilty for having to brush them off, and I often need to sneak away to an undiscovered spot during work hours to avoid being interrupted. However, I always try to compensate by being fully present and available to my family whenever I'm not working.

- **STAYING UP TO DATE AND CATCHING UP ON ADMINISTRATIVE TASKS SO THEY DON'T PILE UP.** This involves answering my current emails and texts *every single day*. If I allowed them to pile up, they would easily overwhelm me in just a few days. I avoid writing lengthy responses, preferring to offer a few kind words to show I care enough to respond promptly. This is critical for any life responsibility that tends to build up and become overwhelming if you don't stay caught up on a daily basis.

A Full Serving of Practice

When we set our sights on achieving overly ambitious goals—like cleaning our oceans, making our streets safe, or eradicating poverty—it's easy to feel overwhelmed. These grand visions can overwhelm and paralyze us, making it difficult to take even the smallest step forward. The enormity of such challenges may feel insurmountable, leading to a sense of hopelessness that freezes us in our tracks. This is why it's crucial to break down monumental objectives into manageable, bite-sized pieces. Rather than seeing our goals as a single feast to consume in one sitting, we can transform them into a series of smaller, bite-sized portions. This approach creates a menu of mini-tasks that feel less intimidating and allow us to savor steady progress one bite at a time.

Focusing on these smaller actions allows us to stay present and engaged rather than becoming overwhelmed by the big picture. Each mini-task completed brings us a step closer to our ultimate vision. By accomplishing and celebrating these small victories, we maintain our momentum and motivation, gradually bridging the gap between where we are now and where we aspire to be. In this way, we can turn our dreams into reality, taking meaningful strides toward our goals without succumbing to the weight of their enormity. Just as a great recipe comes together ingredient by ingredient, progress is built one small step at a time.

Chew on This . . .

Try this **Bite-by-Bite** exercise to feel less overwhelmed while making steady progress toward meaningful change.

- **DEFINE YOUR VISION:** Set the ultimate goal or dream you wish to achieve (e.g., help eradicate poverty).

- **CARVE IT UP:** Break the large goal into smaller, doable actions with a visual checklist. Ask yourself, "What's one little thing I can do today that moves me closer to my goal?"

- **FOCUS SOLELY ON ONE BITE AT A TIME:** Commit to completing that one action *only*, without thinking about any other aspects of the larger goal. No matter how small, finish the task. Even sending one email, making one phone call, or writing one sentence of a novel counts.

- **REWARD THE WINS:** Celebrate your progress and effort by checking that action off your list and feeling a sense of pride at your small yet mighty accomplishment.

- **KEEP ADDING INGREDIENTS:** Keep moving forward, one small task at a time, while applauding your progress every step of the way.

DETACHING FROM YOUR UNHEALTHY EGO

An unhealthy ego is characterized by defensiveness, rigidity, and a fear of failure, stifling creativity and openness to feedback. In contrast, a healthy ego embraces humility, adaptability, and a willingness to learn, fostering a supportive environment for innovation and collaboration. Many claim they want to be creative inventors, but if their motivations stem from an unhealthy ego, they will fear rejection and not getting the accolades they deserve, and they will lack the patience necessary for growth. This ego craves attention, needing to be seen as unique and superior, while perceiving others as threats. It personalizes criticism and is easily offended, perpetually dissatisfied, and constantly seeking the next reward, which fosters chronic frustration and insecurity. Fearful of change, an unhealthy ego generates excuses and limiting beliefs, avoiding taking the risks essential to creativity. Driven by a need for certainty and safety, it rejects questioning and views the unknown as dangerous. In contrast, a Start-from-Scratch mentality requires a healthy ego, as it begins with a completely empty pot and no recipe for guidance. It revels in not knowing, not controlling, and having no idea how the concoction will turn out! Innovation rises out of *no-thingness*!

Story Nugget

We recently wrapped up a round of investor meetings for Lifelines. One positive outcome of the process was the opportunity to share our vision with groups of savvy individuals. It was fascinating to see what resonated with them and what didn't. We genuinely enjoyed telling our story and having our audience express excitement about our successes to date and the future opportunities ahead.

However, one group was particularly critical. They compiled a comprehensive list of concerns, many of which were directed at me and my product development process. Their worries included our tendency to jump too quickly from category to category, not leveraging the intellectual property we had already developed, and failing to drive enough repeat business with existing customers—factors that can significantly impact exit multiples. I was completely taken aback by their comments, as I had never considered the speed of our product launches or the multiples we might achieve at a future exit.

These critiques were a blow to my ego. I felt enraged that the group would judge me so harshly, especially since I had successfully demonstrated my capabilities in building M&D. For several days, I complained to Doug, venting, "How dare they say such things about me! Who do they think they are?" My unhealthy ego was truly bruised.

However, as I distanced myself from my ego reactions and let their comments digest over the next few days, I realized that many of their points were quite insightful and held valuable lessons for our future. In fact, three days after that meeting, I felt compelled to reassess my entire product development strategy. I recognized the need to slow down on certain new categories and focus more intently on the existing products that could drive repeat business and build customer loyalty. Once I was able to depersonalize the experience and respond, rather than react, to their feedback, I saw that their suggestions were constructive and aimed at helping Lifelines reach its full potential. It felt empowering to take them to heart and rethink our entire product development process, integrating those learnings into our strategy!

A Taste of Practice

Your personal practice to detach from the unhealthy ego may include:

- **CULTIVATING SELF-AWARENESS** and learning how to create distance between the ego and the true self. Learn to recognize when your ego is being reactive with judgment or attachment and when you are personalizing interactions or experiences and acting from ego-driven desires, like a fear of rejection, a need for validation, and a desire for superiority. It is through this self-distancing that you can better respond rather than react.

- **SHIFTING THE FOCUS FROM THINKING ABOUT AND FOCUSING ON YOURSELF** to thinking about and focusing on others. When we can transcend ourselves and connect to others, we reduce our self-centered thinking and connect to the larger realm of humanity.

- **LISTENING TO FEEDBACK** and being open to others' opinions to become less rigidly attached to your personal beliefs. Considering other perspectives lifts you outside your own and helps you understand new and different ways of thinking.

- **BEING HONEST ABOUT BOTH YOUR STRENGTHS AND WEAKNESSES** and learning how to cultivate ultimate humility. Humility allows us to recognize our humanness and understand that all humans have limitations. We must see that mistakes are opportunities for growth, not threats to our ego.

- **ENSURING THAT YOUR ACTIONS AND DECISIONS ARE DRIVEN BY YOUR CORE VALUES,** not your unhealthy ego. This way, your actions align with your values, and your unhealthy ego's motivations don't have a place in how you operate in the world.

- **LETTING GO OF THE NEED FOR CONTROL OF ALL SITUATIONS AND OUTCOMES** and trying to embrace uncertainty, unknowing, and the imperfection that comes with being human.

- **PRACTICING GRATITUDE AND APPRECIATION** for what you have rather than bemoaning what you don't have and always seeking more. This helps shift your focus away from unhealthy, ego-driven desires to achieve more and always be better. Every night before I close my eyes, I recollect my "three sweet spots" for that day, highlighting the occurrences that were especially meaningful and made it worthwhile. They allow me to put a final dusting of powdered sugar on a perfectly baked cake, depositing those gifts into my memory bank.

I then close out the day with a smile rather than going to sleep worrying about everything I neglected to do or still need to do tomorrow.

A Full Serving of Practice

Detaching from an unhealthy ego begins with becoming aware of its destructive patterns through cultivating self-awareness. You can enhance your self-awareness by spending just a few minutes each day reflecting on or journaling about your reactions to various situations. Pay attention to which ones you personalize—those instances where your ego reacts defensively. Consider why this is happening. Often, these triggers trace back to events in childhood that you didn't fully understand or process. You may have been left feeling hurt but never investigated the reasons behind those feelings. As an adult, you may find yourself reacting in the same way you did as a child during those incidents.

If you can explore and comprehend why you react in a certain way, understanding that these events are often based on past events rather than present situations, you can reframe those triggers. For example, instead of thinking, *No one respects my ideas and opinions*, you can shift to a healthier and more realistic truth, like *I wasn't listened to as a child and felt disrespected, but that doesn't mean I am being disrespected now!* Creativity flourishes when you adopt a growth mindset that values a love of learning and encourages questioning assumptions, trying new activities, and exploring fresh ideas. This mindset also recognizes that opportunities exist everywhere, even in the bleakest of experiences, and views all lived experiences as chances for growth.

Detaching from your unhealthy ego also entails accepting that feedback is essential to improving your ideas. You must believe that others' input can be valuable and be willing to change your approach based on those insights. Soliciting feedback from peers and mentors involves active listening without interrupting, asking clarifying questions, and understanding different perspectives. This process fosters empathy, which is key to maintaining a healthy ego and creating more intuitive products! Lastly, when situations don't go as planned, detaching from your ego is essential for honest self-reflection. Analyzing what went wrong, why it happened, and what you can learn and change for next time is necessary to improve your ideas and expand your mind.

Chew on This . . .

Try this **Cooking with Clarity** exercise to help cultivate self-awareness, build resilience, and nurture a healthier relationship with your ego.

- **DAILY TASTE TEST:** Set aside five minutes at the end of each day to write down or ponder situations where you became defensive or felt hurt. Ask yourself, "Did I take this too personally?"

- **PINPOINT THE FLAVOR:** Analyze one of those situations and ask, "Why did this *really* bother me? Did it remind me of an experience from the past?"

- **SWEETEN THE DISH:** Challenge your initial reaction and replace it with a healthier perspective. For example, instead of saying, "No one cares about me," try "Although I may have felt unheard in the past, it doesn't define the present." Highlight one or two current examples that disprove your initial reaction and counter your flawed mindset.

- **OFFER TASTE TESTS:** At least once a week, ask someone you trust to offer feedback on your concept or initiative.

Practice active listening without interrupting or asking clarifying questions, and thank them for their input.

- **ENHANCE THE DISH:** Take one piece of helpful feedback and incorporate it into your existing concept. Then, when something doesn't go as you expected, ask yourself three questions: What went wrong? What can I learn from this? How will I do things differently next time?

cherry on top
DEVELOPING A START-FROM-SCRATCH MENTALITY

Starting fresh with an empty pot and no recipe takes courage, but it's the key to creating something truly aligned with your ever-evolving goals and values. This approach encourages experimentation, transforming challenges into opportunities to learn, grow, and innovate. Instead of viewing obstacles as roadblocks, see them as essential ingredients that refine your strategies and inspire your creativity. Remember, every groundbreaking creation starts with the willingness to let go of the past and embrace the unknown!

2

GATHER YOUR INGREDIENTS

Diving Deep into Your Area of Intrigue (AOI) and Exploring Your Passions

To create amazing recipes that represent your end products and services, you need to begin by gathering all sorts of varied ingredients. These original recipes don't necessitate any initial preparation or shopping list ahead of time because you're starting from scratch without any recipe. Ingredients will surface organically when you follow your curiosity and engage in a multitude of life experiences. The only requirement at this stage of the process is to take part in as many diverse activities as possible as well as reading, learning, and accessing knowledge in whatever way naturally sparks your interest. This will allow you to gather the freshest, most delicious, intriguing, and ripest ingredients possible.

The more ingredients you gather the better, as a diverse selection will give you more inventive recipe options down the road. Your most salient ingredients will often emerge when you are inspired by something you weren't aware of ahead of time, whether it's an experience, place, activity, teacher, role model, book, object, or subject that expands your horizons and sparks inspiration. It's those moments of discovery that reveal new possibilities and creative pathways you never knew existed. This capacity to amass ingredients comes from *being fully present in an engaged, active state with the deliberate goal of following your interests wherever they lead.*

The most critical components of the ingredient-gathering process are optimizing for intrigue level, being an utterly indiscriminate gatherer, using negative experiences as crucial ingredients for new recipes, striving to remain in your heart (not your critical mind), and becoming more intrinsically motivated. I'll get into these in more detail here.

Optimizing for Intrigue Level

When collecting ingredients, you should always and only follow what truly piques your interest and captivates your attention. This is a critical part of self-discovery. The activities that organically spark your curiosity have the best chance of leading you to a life passion and an original recipe. Optimize for the level of *intrigue* (I love the word "intrigue" because it means "to arouse the curiosity or interest of and fascinate"[1]) by engaging in and giving all kinds of different activities a chance so they can show you what they're really like.

You never know when or where your essence will be kindled by someone or something, and you should deliberately search for and unearth ingredients across as many areas of art and culture as possible. It has always been a shock to me what unusual things fascinate me! And those incredible experiences *frequently* come when I do something that I was initially reluctant to try, either because I believed nothing worthwhile would come of it or because I was too scared to do it!

Being an Utterly Indiscriminate Gatherer

When gathering ingredients, it is essential to be spontaneous, unpredictable, and utterly indiscriminate in which ingredients you gather (I also love this word, as it means "done at random *without* careful judgment").[2] If you are engaging in the most effective gathering process, you will be operating haphazardly, with no idea why you are gathering certain ingredients other than that they fascinate you and you are simply following your curiosity. Therefore, most ingredients you collect will be general in nature, and you will have no idea if, how, or when they will be used in a recipe. They will simply get shelved in the huge kitchen pantry of your mind, where they will remain available for potential future use. And that's exactly what must happen since this is the unknowing part of the process, where you remain open to everything with every ingredient readily available for a future recipe. You're simply in gathering mode and stocking your pantry with as many wide-ranging ingredients as possible.

Don't allow your mind to become tethered to any one ingredient or category of ingredients. Explore all kinds of things and keep your mind completely open. Keep questioning your existing beliefs and speculate about how you can think and do things differently. Remember, you are an indiscriminate explorer without constraints or rules, yet you understand that blending ingredients from multiple areas of interest will ultimately yield more inventive combinations and mouth-watering recipes. That means some ingredients will ultimately be used in product recipes, and some will not. However, you *can never* know ahead of time which ingredients will be most helpful to your innovations, so you must go through the entire process first!

Using Negative Experiences as Crucial Ingredients for New Recipes

Our natural tendency is to try to immediately erase or repress all setbacks, including troubling experiences, mistakes, outbursts, triggers, missteps, failures, and imperfections. However, these faults must all be treated as fresh ingredients that either get chopped up and put into an already-simmering pot or placed on a pantry shelf for storage. These myriad "failures" represent the most critical elements of the creative process since, with time to reflect, they provide brand-new information on why something didn't work. Once these failures are depersonalized by transcending your wounded ego and conscious mind, then giving them time to blend with other relevant ingredients, they will yield entirely new combinations and incredible insights on the path forward. In essence, you're keeping the peels and stems from your pristine vegetables and, instead of throwing them in the trash, tossing them right back into the pot to enhance your recipe's depth and flavor!

Striving to Remain in Your Heart, Not Your Critical Mind

In gathering mode, you must stay completely in your heart and not your critical mind. You're simply stocking your pantry with as many varied ingredients as possible. Here, we cannot allow our minds to judge or question the purpose or outcome of our gathering. This is about experiencing, not analyzing. Explore all kinds of interests, and keep your mind completely open to discovering something extraordinary and new. Remember, the more ingredients you can unearth and collect, the more opportunities you will have down the road to combine them into unique recipes. In children, we would simply call this activity *play*—pursued for nothing more than the joy of doing it!

Becoming More Intrinsically Motivated

Intrinsic motivation comes out of supreme self-awareness. It's an innate knowing that you are involved in the activity because of the internal reward generated from the work itself rather than extrinsic rewards like fame, fortune, and money.[3] When you are intrinsically motivated, the work becomes autotelic—a Greek term meaning that the activity is an end in itself, much like play.[4] How do you access more intrinsic motivation? Follow your curiosity and engage in activities that help you achieve an optimal level of arousal and set your heart on fire! They cannot be too challenging since that will create frustration or anxiety and lead you to quit, and they cannot be too easy, as that will make them boring, dull, and uninspiring, again causing you to want to quit.

A Taste of Practice

Your personal practice to stay in gathering mode and amass as many intriguing ingredients as possible may include:

- **BECOMING MORE AWARE OF YOUR REACTIVE BEHAVIOR** and noticing how often you close the door to new experiences. Your unhealthy ego convinces you that the experience will be negative when it has no idea what surprises and delight it may hold. The next time someone invites you to go somewhere or do something unusual, *say yes*! Push yourself to try *one* new experience every week, especially if it's something that makes you fearful or falls outside your comfort zone. Endeavor to approach these new experiences with an open and positive mindset. Often, you will be pleasantly surprised by the end result!

- **REPEATING THE PHRASE "COLLECT, DON'T INSPECT"** to remind yourself that this part of the process is about being entirely in the verb of exploring and discovering, not the noun of locking in on the ultimate destination. Visualize yourself running through a cavernous supermarket with a bottomless shopping cart and innumerable ingredients to throw into that cart. At this stage, no one is forcing you to choose among the plethora of fascinating options within your grasp—take as many as you'd like as often as you'd like!

- **CHALLENGING YOURSELF TO EXPLORE NEW INTERESTS** by taking up new hobbies or learning new skills that broaden your horizons. I continually create goals related to the new activities I want to try or experiences I wish to have, and then I hold myself accountable to complete them. You might also consider having an accountability buddy who can help ensure that you stay on track with your goals. Related to this is also attempting things that terrify you. This is the only way you'll grow outside your comfort zone and demonstrate tremendous courage in rising above your fear! Physical challenges petrify me, and I recently went on a twelve-mile e-biking tour in the mountains. For those joining me, this experience was quite ordinary. But for me, it was incredibly challenging and truly satisfying to conquer. I completed the tour and enjoyed it immensely, giving myself a well-deserved pat on the back for my courage!

- **GREETING PEOPLE YOU DON'T ALREADY KNOW.** No matter where you are, say hello to the people around you, as it can be as delightful as opening a box of chocolates. I take walks multiple times each day, and greeting people from different backgrounds with fresh perspectives has broadened my horizons and helped me forge friendships I never would have imagined. Developing these connections with people of all ages has given me multitudes of fascinating insights as well as a much stronger sense of community!

- **TRAVELING MORE AND MOVING BEYOND YOUR COMFORTABLE SURROUNDINGS.** If you have the resources to do so, visit new regions and immerse yourself in different experiences and cultures. You can also do this within your own town or city. I took a comparative religion class in college, and we were tasked with immersing ourselves in another religion. I chose Southern Baptist and found it to be one of the most eye-opening experiences of my life, providing lessons that I still utilize today!

- **KEEPING A JOURNAL AND TAKING TIME TO REFLECT ON YOUR EXPERIENCES,** documenting what you've learned and the insights you've gained, and detailing how you've changed as a result. I also take innumerable photos to help me capture fleeting experiences, fondly recall them afterward, and share these memorable adventures with others!

- **CONTINUOUSLY EXPANDING YOUR KNOWLEDGE BASE AND PERSPECTIVE** by reading, taking courses, listening to podcasts, and attending workshops or lectures that interest you. I took an independent study in logotherapy (healing through meaning) with a professor in Canada, and two years later, I was thrilled to have a certificate in logotherapy coaching that I utilize every day!

- **SUPPORTING CAUSES THAT PIQUE YOUR INTEREST** to gain a sense of belonging and meaning or engaging in volunteer work and community service projects that help you entrench your roots in your community. Doug and I were recently involved in a local effort to stop a treasured community grocery and deli from getting razed and turned into another luxury home. It was preserved and officially designated a community gathering place. Seeing it packed with families gives us a tremendous sense of fulfillment and pride!

Story Nugget

When I was younger, I would never have had the courage to write my heroes and ask if they would consider speaking with me; I would have been much too fearful of rejection. But now,

I have adopted the mindset of "What do I have to lose?" Years ago, I became a disciple of Dr. Emmy van Deurzen, a philosopher, psychologist, and existential therapist who has written over thirty books and taught and practiced for five decades. Her works have been translated into several dozen languages, and she serves as president of the existential movement. I longed for the chance to tell her how she positively impacted my life and ask her a host of questions about life's meaning that I had never felt comfortable discussing with anyone else.

I decided to email Dr. van Deurzen a note requesting a Zoom chat with her. For context, I had previously written similar notes to other individuals I admired without ever receiving a response. Yet she replied almost immediately, agreeing to speak with me. That was four years ago, and since then, we've had regular monthly conversations that have profoundly influenced my life. Her wisdom resonates deeply with me, allowing me to feel okay in this topsy-turvy world. I honestly cannot imagine the void that would still exist without her guidance and mentorship. And all this came about because I took a risk and reached out to her!

A Full Serving of Practice

It's instinctual to avoid activities that push you out of your comfort zone because your body is wired for homeostasis and to crave safety. However, some of your most valuable insights will emerge from stepping outside those familiar boundaries. Gradually building the courage to try new things is possible with a few simple steps.

Start by acknowledging your fears and recognizing what holds you back—whether it's a fear of the unknown, failure, judgment, or all three. Reflect on past experiences where fear stopped you; understanding these triggers will help you address them more effectively. Use mindfulness techniques like deep breathing and meditation to manage anxiety, and visualize yourself navigating new experiences effectively to lessen fear and boost confidence.

Begin by taking on small, low-risk challenges that stretch your boundaries without overwhelming you. Join a group, attend a new social event, or try a different hobby, and celebrate your courage in taking these steps. Keep in mind that not all new experiences will yield positive outcomes, but each one is an opportunity for growth. Insights can arise from both successes and setbacks, enriching your creative process.

Keep a journal to record your experiences, noting how they felt and what you learned. Reflect on what worked, what didn't, and why, then keep pushing yourself to try again, even after less-than-ideal experiences. Share your journey with others and surround yourself with supportive individuals who encourage exploration. Each new experience broadens your skill set and knowledge, fueling your creativity. The more you explore, the more diverse your sources of inspiration become, leading to richer ingredients and more innovation in your work. Embrace the journey of trying new things; it is vital to unlock your full creative potential.

Chew on This . . .

Try this **Taste of the Unknown** exercise to become more adept at stepping outside your comfort zone and savoring the richness of growth and courage.

- **ONE NEW DISH A DAY:** Commit to trying one simple, unfamiliar activity each day, like listening to a new genre of music on your walk or way to work. Write it down the night before to set the intention.

- **SAVOR THE FLAVOR OF FEAR:** When fear arises, ask yourself, "What's the worst that can happen?" Then ponder, "What could I learn/how can I grow from this experience?"

- **TAKE A NIBBLE OF BRAVERY:** To close each day, highlight even your smallest acts of bravery. Keep a courage diary where you transcribe these wins and the insights they helped spark.

- **CREATE A WEEKLY MENU:** Select a larger challenge for the week that is truly exciting but also scary and pushes you just beyond your existing comfort zone. Break that larger goal into smaller steps that you can complete one at a time each day.

- **COMPILE YOUR INGREDIENT LIST:** At the end of each week, identify three insights or lessons that came from stepping out and trying something new. How will you utilize these lessons to tackle bigger challenges in the weeks ahead?

DISCOVER YOUR MOST CAPTIVATING INGREDIENTS AND AREA OF INTRIGUE (AOI)

Some ingredients captivate your senses with their tantalizing flavors, filling you with joy and drawing you in with their deep resonance. This happens when you approach the gathering process with a curious, playful spirit, much like a child exploring their world. Once an ingredient has tickled your taste buds and sparked a craving, you'll find it irresistible and you'll become passionate about exploring it further. In fact, when this occurs, you will know, with every ounce of your being, that you must further develop your knowledge of or skill in this area of intrigue (AOI), engaging in it as often and as intensely as you can. This moment of memorable, dynamic contact with an activity of fascination or field of endeavor is a *real, documented effect* that psychologist Howard Gardner calls a "crystallizing experience." Gardner explains, "It's like experiencing love at first sight with the potential of activating long-term changes in perspective and self-awareness. This moment catalyzes people to say, 'This is the real me; this is what I would like to do, to devote my life to, going forward!' Ultimately, the individual and the activity become one and the same, and we see our true selves and our highest potential reflected in this passion/dream."[5]

The crystallizing experience is so life-altering that the feelings remaining after that moment cannot ever be eliminated or forgotten. In truth, it takes this level of enthusiasm to intrinsically invest deep attention and focus on your AOI for decades to follow! However, Gardner adds, "It is not possible to identify a crystallizing experience at the moment of its occurrence. Only retrospectively, after the individual's behavior in the post-crystallizing period has been observed, is it possible to single out an experience as having crystallized ensuing activities."[6]

The insights that emerge from these crystallizing experiences are far too valuable to be left untouched or discarded. Like the ripest, most flavorful ingredients, they shouldn't be shelved in the mind's pantry. Instead, they deserve a place on your creative stove, marinating on back burners as you dive deeper into exploring your AOI and gathering additional key elements for your recipe.

What If You Cannot Zero In on a Single AOI, Problem to Solve, or Concept?

It turns out that the biggest barrier to originality isn't creativity and generating ideas; it's sifting through those ideas to select one to focus on. That's because there's a shortage of people who excel at convergent thinking and choosing the right novel and practical idea to act on.[7] Some people can't tell the difference between good and bad ideas until it's too late and they've wasted lots of time.

Conversely, they may have many ideas but don't know how to sort through them to determine which one is most likely to become a business or product that sells like hotcakes. They become paralyzed by asking, "Which idea will be best?" and keep spinning ideas around without turning them into something tangible. Or they find an AOI but quickly move on to the next, never taking the time to dive deep and fully immerse themselves in it. To use a food analogy, they remain *nibblers* rather than *savorers*.

Convergent thinking is the analytical capacity and ability to sift through divergent ideas and recognize which ones are worth pursuing and which are not. It's a discerning capacity that requires a healthy measure of critical thinking and good judgment, as an ordered analysis is required to be self-critical. Those with high intelligence often fall more into convergent thinking because they are quick decision-makers who can think more narrowly and quickly home in to determine one right answer. Convergent thinking involves the brain's left hemisphere, responsible for planning, structuring, logic, and analysis. Divergent thinkers, on the other hand, are idea generators. They have the ability to conceive a wide range of ideas and possible solutions, often branching out in unexpected or unconventional directions. Divergent thinking requires originality, flexibility, and the capacity to make connections between seemingly unrelated concepts. This leads to innovative and diverse outcomes.[8]

If you stay in brainstorming (divergent thinking) mode and keep throwing out new ideas, you will never actually converge on an area of specialization, define a target market (the segment of consumers who best align with your product/service and are most inclined to purchase or utilize it), and understand what differentiates your concept from the competition. And if you don't define a specific niche or target market, your products may try to be everything to everyone. Narrowing the market through convergent thinking often helps you speak more directly and passionately to those you are trying to serve.

When faced with a complex problem or an abundance of enticing solutions, it is easy to become overwhelmed. This can lead you to become frozen into inaction, selecting a less important problem to focus on or selecting an inferior solution that doesn't solve the real problem.[9] To be a successful entrepreneur, it's crucial that you cultivate the ability to synthesize a great deal of information and focus on what really matters. You must discard the irrelevant pieces as you refine the idea, digging deeper into the relevant information and letting one specific problem become dominant. Although divergent thinking is essential in the early stages of gathering ingredients and exploring AOIs, narrowing your focus through convergent thinking—identifying the most important problem and zeroing in on a sweet-spot idea that will drive success—is critical to building a viable venture.

Story Nugget

I've always thought about successful entrepreneurship as similar to the story "Goldilocks and the Three Bears." It's about finding that optimal balance—too much of one thing and you can veer off track, but the right blend can make all the difference.

In my mentoring experience, the entrepreneurs who truly succeed strike this "just right" blend between divergent and convergent thinking. In the food sense, they can find "the gooey center" of ideation. At first, they can generate a broad range of wild, ambitious, and creative concepts that are exciting and full of potential. But here's where the magic happens: they don't stay in that dreaming phase. They are able to change gears and narrow in on one idea that's not just interesting but actionable. They're able to refine and shape their thinking from the abstract into something real—a tangible product or service that can be designed and brought to life.

I've talked with enough entrepreneurs to know, almost instantly, who will turn their ideas into reality and who won't. It's in the way they speak about their ventures, the way they bounce between ideas and action, and—most importantly—whether they can both *dream* and *focus*. I've met many entrepreneurs who are like squirrels endlessly chasing acorns, full of enthusiasm and eagerly scampering from one idea to the next. However, it soon becomes clear that they are unable to commit to anything long enough to transform it into something impactful. They have lots of energy and enthusiasm, but without the ability to focus, they're just a whirlwind of potential that never materializes into anything concrete.

Likewise, I often meet with founders who converge too quickly on one idea without ever fully exploring other possibilities, rushing to narrow their focus before taking the time to contemplate the full range of what's possible. That rush mentality may tempt them to dive straight into execution, but without taking the time to consider the broader scope, these entrepreneurs tend to miss out on opportunities that could make their ventures truly extraordinary.

The best entrepreneurs are the ones who are able to effortlessly move between *imagining* and *doing*. They're able to play with ideas, explore possibilities, and then slow down long enough to choose the one that's just right—just like Goldilocks finding that perfect bowl of porridge. It's a delicate dance: generating a wealth of creative ideas, then narrowing them down to the one that has the most potential to be built into something real and genuinely impactful. If you excel in one of these areas of thinking but not the other, it is essential to have a partner or employee on your team who can complement your abilities and round out these necessary skills.

DEVOTE YOURSELF TO LEARNING MORE ABOUT YOUR AOI

So far, I have stressed that the key to conceiving amazing recipes is gathering a wide variety of ingredients in as many distinct areas as possible. But just as importantly, the more obscure the domains you dive into, the better! Charles Darwin collected hundreds of plant specimens for decades all over the world until he visited the Galápagos Islands and found that plant species and animals differed from island to island, even though they were relatively close in proximity. This was when he began forming his revolutionary ideas about evolution. He also spent an entire decade studying barnacle taxonomy and years collecting beetle species simply because he was following his AOIs! Steve Jobs became fascinated with type font, which led to the creation of a revolutionary new computer. Temple Grandin became obsessed with studying livestock, which ultimately led her to design more humane livestock handling systems, and Julia Child became fascinated with French cuisine, which inspired her to simplify difficult cooking techniques and share her findings with the masses. Embracing unconventional interests can spark lifelong careers driven by a passion for exploration and discovery.

The key aspects of diving into your AOI are putting in your time, understanding what it takes to become a master chef, entering a flow state, and becoming increasingly fascinated by your AOI as you grow your knowledge base. Let's look at each of these points in a bit more detail.

Putting in Your Time

Once you discover a problem to solve or an AOI you'd like to dive into, you need to put hours of serious time into learning more about it—not just because you must but because you are obsessed with gaining more knowledge and you find it incredibly fun. Remember, patience is at the heart of entrepreneurship! Immerse yourself so deeply in every aspect of the area that you absorb its processes, rules, and skills until they are seamlessly integrated into your repository of knowledge. Over many hours of study, the rules of the AOI (e.g., medicine, health care, education, science, technology, finance, entertainment, media, toys) become part of who you are, and you can view the whole picture with total clarity.

This is an ideal blend of instinct and rational, conscious, and unconscious processes. Through intense focus and absorption in your

AOI over extended periods, your mind will become immersed with its knowledge until it can take in no more and you understand every single aspect involved in what you're studying. Your brain will become like a kitchen sponge that can absorb no additional fluid. That's the point when all your gathered ingredients are internalized, and instead of focusing on the individual parts, you develop an intuitive sense of the whole. All those separate ingredients will merge into a unified whole, and you'll perceive only the complete, integrated result.[10]

Understanding What It Takes to Become a Master Chef

As you hone your skills, you will also begin to fully understand and integrate the information or skills you've acquired so they become a natural part of how you think and act. This is what makes you "a master chef" in your AOI, so you'll naturally know if you're doing a good job or if you need to modify or improve your skills. This aspect is an essential part of becoming an expert because it enables you to critically assess your performance and give yourself feedback as you engage in the activity. Without taking the time to internalize what skills masters need to sharpen or what an exceptional product/service looks like in your category, you'll never be able to innately know or assess whether it's going well, and you won't be able to engage in continual self-improvement.[11] In summary, the practice of becoming a master chef involves:

- **COMMITTING TO CONTINUOUS LEARNING:** Deeply study and immerse yourself in your AOI to build on your already growing foundation of knowledge.

- **INTEGRATING AND INTERNALIZING SKILLS:** Practice until your knowledge and techniques become second nature.

- **SEEKING FEEDBACK:** Get input from mentors, peers, and experts to gain new perspectives on your progress and refine your skills.

- **ENGAGING IN SELF-ASSESSMENT:** Reflect on your performance to identify both your strengths and areas for improvement.

- **ADAPTING AND IMPROVING:** Use feedback and self-assessment to adjust and modify your approach.

- **REPEATING AND EVOLVING:** Continuously hone your skills and refine your techniques to maintain high standards over time.

Entering a Flow State

If you fully immerse yourself in your AOI, you may experience peak enjoyment and performance and enter flow state. Flow state is a mental state characterized by intense focus, clear goals and immediate feedback, balance between challenge and skill, loss of self-consciousness, transformation of time, and intrinsic motivation.[12] In this harmonious state, a person experiences a perfect balance between the challenge of the task and their skill level, leading to a sense of effortlessness and deep satisfaction. Here, attention can be freely invested to achieve a person's goals because there is no disorder to straighten out and no threat for the self to defend against. Those who regularly enter flow state are able to develop a stronger, more confident self because more of their psychic energy has been successfully invested in goals they have chosen to pursue.[13]

Offering yourself continuous feedback is necessary to experience a flow state because it provides the motivation to continue pushing forward and engaging in the work despite the many challenges blocking your path. When you can clearly see that your skills are improving, you will become intrinsically motivated to continue putting in the effort to hone them. Once you have mastered the extensive knowledge that defines expertise, you'll be poised to act instinctively and bring your unique qualities into the AOI.[14]

However, it's important to recognize that flow state cannot be pursued directly as an end goal. It must emerge naturally as a byproduct of fully immersing yourself in an AOI and dedicating the time and effort necessary to achieve proficiency. When it arrives, it's like a spoonful of honey—sweet, satisfying, and the perfect reward for your hard work.

Story Nugget

My personal experience of flow state has felt nothing short of magical. When I was younger, I didn't know the term "flow state" and believed I heard "angels singing" whenever I was pulled into that transcendent realm. It was as if I had ascended to a new dimension aglow with white light, celestial music, puffy clouds, and angels—a place as beautiful as heaven itself. In that space, everything was infused with an ethereal white radiance, and I was floating in that calm, peaceful, boundless expanse of white space. Everything else remained suspended in stillness, but I had infinite freedom to create without any sense of restriction. It was the ultimate blend of liberation, serenity, and limitless possibility.

In the hush and openness of that world, I felt empowered to craft anything my mind could conjure, unhindered by constraints or guardrails. Truly, it seemed as if I stepped outside the normal flow of time. I was fully immersed in the present and aligned with my true essence, effortlessly doing exactly what I was meant to do. And I didn't want to be anywhere else but right there.

One challenge with entering this state is that I have come to crave it so deeply. When I'm in that moment, I never want it to end. I become completely immersed, so consumed by the creative process that I lose all desire to sleep, eat, or do anything else. Nothing matters other than staying in that flow.

Becoming Increasingly Fascinated by Your AOI Through Learning More

If a particular AOI truly becomes your passion, you will grow increasingly enthusiastic and enamored with it as you learn more. In fact, you may become so fixated that you find yourself thinking about it every waking moment of the day. At this point, it has sunk its teeth into you to such an extent that it won't release its grip, becoming part of your central nervous system. This level of passion and engagement is a strong litmus test for the long-term staying power of your AOI, as passion is a key ingredient at the heart of entrepreneurship!

As you become further enthralled and dig deeper and deeper into your AOI, you will develop your own unique form of engagement that resonates and is a true reflection of who you are. But you will only achieve this level of immersion if you joyfully put in the effort. To cultivate intrinsic motivation—the drive fueled by internal rewards rather than external ones—you must have an intense passion for and absorption in your AOI. You will be propelled by an inner force so powerful that it cannot even be articulated. Developing this innate drive is also necessary as an entrepreneur because it will give you the determination to keep fighting in the face of the challenges and roadblocks that will inevitably arise during your entrepreneurial journey. Passion alone can never replace intense, hard work, but this elusive combination of hard work plus an intense love of your AOI is essential to becoming a master chef in your field and having the capacity to innovate successfully over a lengthy time span.

However, becoming completely enmeshed in your AOI has a fine line. Although studying the minutest of details will bring you closer to developing a deeper, more intuitive understanding of the true nature of your AOI, you must be mindful enough to not get so caught up in the tiny details that you lose sight of the big picture. It's that ability to step back with a wider perspective that generates groundbreaking insights. Start by focusing on the small details until you've fully absorbed the knowledge, then gradually shift away from those details to the bigger picture.

I crafted the following mantra to remain mindful of this concept of learning the rules of your AOI until they've become woven into your being, then abandoning them as your intuition takes over so you can freely innovate:

> Master the rules
> *So you know them by heart*
> Then reject them as fools
> *Free to forge novel art*

If you fall into the snare of "rush mentality" and race through the ingredient-gathering phase of the creative process, you may never have that "crystallizing experience" of discovering an AOI. Therefore, you may never develop an unstoppable drive to dig in and learn everything there is to learn about it and build your level of expertise. Rush mentality may have you embarking on a desperate search to find "that good idea" rather than allowing the idea to come to you organically from fully immersing yourself in an AOI. This may then lead you to solve a personal problem rather than a larger societal problem, frustration, or unmet need *or* contrive an idea based on what you *think* others want and push it out into the market.

It's critical to take the time to truly understand what your target consumers are seeking. Otherwise, you may end up going down the wrong path rather than intuitively allowing the concept to unfold. In these instances, there will be no real demand for the product or service you've created. People will be much more apt to spend their hard-earned money on your recipe if it satisfies an *existing*, significant need rather than a new need you're trying to convince them that they have!

STAYING FOCUSED, INVESTING TIME, AND EXPLORING UNIQUE INTERESTS

I have needed to embrace patience, focus, and continually fight against my personal urge to rush and churn out one product after another. Over time, I learned how to immerse myself deeply in the product I was creating, treating it as if it were the only one that mattered. I would whisper to myself, "Pour your heart and soul into this *one product* and make it the best it can be." I challenged myself to stay present with questions like "What if this is the only product someone ever purchases from M&D? Is this the first impression you want to leave? Does this product experience encapsulate everything you believe in?" I needed to infuse every bit of my passion and authentic purpose into that specific product, ensuring that it embodied my deepest values and aspirations.

Finding the right AOI is key to maintaining focus, and doing so often stems from pursuing a wide range of unique, quirky interests. Many of my offbeat interests and innocent questions led directly to product lines and epiphanies at both M&D and Lifelines. Just a few examples of these are:

- My passion for being a Girl Scout and exploring the outdoors led to a line of M&D adventure toys called Let's Explore.

- My love of making sand desserts as a child using containers and spice jars led to a line of M&D sand food toys.

- My enthusiasm for crafting led to hundreds of innovative crafts for children at M&D and now a crafting line for teens and adults at Lifelines.

- My obsession with collecting shells led to a keepsake M&D product that enables children to affix their treasures in a sand-and-cement base for display.

- A license-plate game I made up as a child for long car trips turned into a formal M&D travel version for families.

- My struggle to break free from rumination led to the discovery that my senses had the capacity to counter stress and induce calm. This inspired the creation of our company Lifelines, which creates innovative sensory immersion tools.

- My enthusiasm for mentoring young entrepreneurs and exploring why some of their ventures succeeded and others didn't inspired me to write this book.

Two other fun examples of quirky pastimes leading to breakthrough ideas are:

- **VELCRO:** Swiss engineer George de Mestral invented Velcro in 1941 after a walk in the woods with his dog. Noticing burrs clinging to his dog's fur, he examined them under a microscope and saw tiny hooks that hooked onto the loops of the hairs. This discovery inspired him to develop Velcro, a hook-and-loop fastening system now used in clothing, shoes, and many other products.[15]

- **MICROWAVE OVEN:** In the 1940s, engineer Percy Spencer was working with radar equipment at Raytheon when he noticed that a candy bar in his pocket had melted. Curious about why this had happened, he discovered that the radar's microwaves had caused the candy to melt. This observation led to the invention of the microwave oven, which transformed cooking methods throughout the world.[16]

Story Nugget

Doug and I were so determined to leave the corporate world behind that we threw ourselves into making children's live-action videotapes by utilizing our existing skills rather than filling an existing market need. Doug, with his background in producing television commercials, felt well-equipped to create the videos, and I, as a songwriter and vocalist, could contribute lyrics and vocals for the soundtracks. While we did tap into a novel and growing category at the time, we overlooked how difficult it would be to market our creation and generate real consumer demand. We didn't realize that to achieve mass awareness, video programs needed to be syndicated on national television to expose them to the target market. Shows like *Barney & Friends* did just that and became *highly* successful, although most others never really gained mass popularity.

Nevertheless, we still managed to widely distribute our video into toy stores. But despite how enthusiastically we encouraged those retailers to expose it to their customers, we couldn't force them to make the sale. Although by sheer tenacity, we were able to develop a profitable business, there just wasn't enough sell-through excitement and repeat orders from toy stores to maintain the intrinsic motivation to keep plugging away.

However, by this point, we had gained a solid understanding of the inner workings of the toy industry and had developed a unique distribution model. It wasn't long before our next idea came to us completely organically. One day, Doug and I were driving and casually reminiscing about our childhoods, discussing our favorite toys and the reasons we loved them. As discussed earlier, that conversation and subsequent investigation led to the creation of our very first category of wooden puzzles, driving decades of successful growth in that segment.

Looking back, our first products were forced to fit into the market and failed to achieve mass acceptance. Fortunately, we recognized the need to pivot just in time, as VHS tapes have since disappeared. Had we remained inflexible and stayed on that path, we would have quickly found ourselves out of business.

BECOMING A MASTER CHEF IN YOUR AREA OF INTRIGUE

For this process to be effective, you must immerse yourself in your problem to solve or AOI so thoroughly that your mind continually contemplates it, even unconsciously, at every available moment. You cannot expect to innovate if you don't *truly* understand your AOI inside and out. It's this intense focus that provides the courage to keep driving forward, taking risks, and overcoming the inevitable roadblocks. However, the reality is that most entrepreneurs aren't patient enough to find an AOI that they're truly passionate about, methodically engage in the work it takes to learn everything about it, and discover their deeper purpose. It's the combination of passion, patience, and the purpose that emerges from these qualities that lies at the heart of entrepreneurship.

If the problem you choose to solve or AOI isn't at the intersection of your passions and talents ("passients") and doesn't make ample use of your unique skills and life experiences, you won't ultimately have the intrinsic motivation, perseverance, and commitment to see it through. No one can sustain creative activity without intense passion for and commitment to understanding their AOI. You must be eager to explore your AOI or problem to solve, no matter how much time it takes.

A Taste of Practice

Your personal practice to invest more time in your AOI may include:

- **DEFINING WHICH AOIs ARE THE MOST IMPORTANT** to you and align with your current values. I have so many areas that fascinate me that I need to be very deliberate about choosing only the *most* salient ones to actively pursue. I then establish clear, achievable goals to keep me focused on hitting specific learning objectives and implement firm deadlines for even these passion projects. That way, I keep on track and consistently progress toward tangible milestones.

- **ALLOCATING SOLID BLOCKS OF TIME TO DEDICATE TO YOUR AOI** and sticking to them. If you cannot find those blocks of time in your calendar, it means you are engaged in too many activities. In that case, you must reduce time spent on nonessential activities and distractions to free up more time for your passions. I do a bimonthly assessment of my activities, asking the simple question "Is this something I am doing out of love or out of obligation?" I start by listing everything I do in a week in order of priority. Next, I actively trim away the tasks at the bottom of the list that don't ignite true passion. If possible, try to optimize your time by delegating non-essential tasks to others. Of course, there will always be responsibilities on your list that must get accomplished, even if you don't absolutely love them. Yet by regularly engaging in this trimming exercise, you will be able to eliminate the activities you don't enjoy, making time for the activities you are *truly* passionate about and that connect you to a genuine sense of purpose!

- **REMEMBERING THAT IT'S NOT ALL OR NOTHING.** Allow for flexibility in how and when you engage in your passions, adapting to your life's ever-changing demands. If you are having a tough week and are unable to make time for your AOI, it doesn't mean you'll never be able to enjoy it again. Give yourself a break and realize that next week can be entirely different! Humans are fallible, and life doesn't generally go as we plan. So try to remain adaptable, and be ready to adjust your schedule and priorities if necessary.

- **EFFECTIVELY OPTIMIZING TIME AND COMBINING AND INTEGRATING AOIs WITH YOUR DAILY ROUTINE.** I love immersing myself in nature, taking walks, and practicing mindfulness, but I also love learning. During one of my daily walks, I listen to meditations or podcasts, engaging two passions simultaneously. I also schedule walking phone-call meetings to combine exercise with work. While driving to appointments, I use the time intentionally—relaxing with uplifting music, learning from inspiring podcasts, or handling obligatory calls and meetings. Even my breaks reflect my passions—whether through nature, music, art, or some form of creativity. You can also incorporate your interests into social activities, such as joining a religious or book group or attending interesting workshops and lectures related to your AOIs. You may also find friends who share similar interests and pursue those activities together to heighten your enjoyment while deepening your relationships.

- **UNDERSTANDING THAT MULTITASKING IS JUST FRAGMENTED ATTENTION AND NOT CONDUCIVE TO MINDFULNESS AND FLOW STATE.** When I am thoroughly engaged in my AOI, I am very intent on eliminating distractions that steal my attention and limit my ability to enter that flow state and attain optimal enjoyment and efficiency. Try to avoid multitasking, and focus on one passion-related activity at a time.

- **SHARING YOUR PASSION PROJECTS WITH FRIENDS AND FAMILY** not only helps gain their support but also adds a layer of accountability. And if you make your descriptions compelling enough, they may even want to join you next time!

A Full Serving of Practice

Most people approach their lives using the peanut-butter approach—spreading their limited resources, time, or energy too thinly across multiple projects, tasks, or initiatives. The more you spread yourself across too many areas, the less effective or impactful each individual task becomes. Your precious attention, time, or resources are divided to the point where none of them receive the full, concentrated effort necessary to deliver meaningful results.

This approach is counter to the heart of entrepreneurship. As a successful entrepreneur, you will need to discover areas that spark your passion, dive into them with supreme focus and patience to become proficient, and allow that engagement to generate creative insights that give your life purpose. Without this deep level of passion, patience, and purpose in an area, success will remain elusive.

To achieve this level of focus, you must continually assess how you spend your time and eliminate any nonessential activities. Start by listing how you spend your time for one week, noting each task and how long you spend on it. Then, create a hierarchy, ranking activities by how much passion they ignite and how essential they are to your family, livelihood, or survival. Remove anything that neither feeds your passion nor supports your survival.

Next, schedule blocks of time dedicated to the activities that matter most. For me, writing this book while building our Lifelines start-up, parenting six children, and serving on multiple boards and initiatives required me to carve out specific time slots with concrete, daily goals. Based on my ever-changing schedule, I decided to work on the book early in the morning or late at night, with the goal of completing five pages each day to meet the production schedule. Otherwise, I knew I would never find the time to complete it.

My schedule also needed to be flexible, as I knew it would continually change. Moreover, I needed to be kind with myself, knowing that creativity naturally ebbs and flows. Some days, my ideas gushed like water, and I effortlessly completed ten or more pages of the book with ease. Other days, I needed to force the words out onto the page, and it was pure agony.

This process of intentionally dedicating time to my priorities has been a game changer. It has allowed me to define the areas where I wish to make significant impact and take daily steps toward achieving those goals. Above all, this approach has built my confidence, showing me that by giving focused attention to my passions, I can single-mindedly propel myself forward and bring new concepts to life that would have never emerged without that commitment.

Chew on This . . .

Try this **Cooking with Purpose** exercise to bring your priorities into focus and savor each task:

- **DISH OF THE DAY:** Before beginning each day, take a few minutes to ask yourself, "What is one thing I can do today that will have the biggest impact on my goals?" Write it down and keep it visible.

- **PROTECT YOUR PREP TIME:** Commit to dedicating one uninterrupted hour each day to a single, high-priority task. Honor and protect this time fiercely so you can remain undistracted and fully immerse yourself in it.

- **TASTE-TEST REFLECTION:** At the end of each day, ask yourself, "Did I focus on the task that truly mattered? If not, what can I alter tomorrow?"

- **SAVOR THE SUBTLE FLAVORS** Appreciate even small steps forward, recognizing that any forward progress is part of achieving your goals.

- **WEEKLY MENU ASSESSMENT:** At the close of each week, assess what worked and what didn't, utilizing these insights to refine your approach and enhance your focus for the upcoming week.

cherry on top
CURATING YOUR FLAVORFUL PANTRY

To cultivate passion, patience, and purpose—the heart of entrepreneurship—take the time to explore what truly intrigues you, even if it feels unconventional. Trust that persistence and steady effort will allow your interests to ripen and bear fruit. Meaningful endeavors often take time to reveal their depth and significance. Following your curiosity and embracing what stirs your heart will drive you to pursue your goals, fostering an authentic sense of purpose. This journey is essential to unlocking your true potential and finding your unique voice.

3

ALLOW YOUR INGREDIENTS TO SIMMER

Taking Time to Spark Insight, Inspiration, and Intuition

Let's return to the metaphor of the creative brain as a bustling commercial kitchen, constantly churning out inventive recipes. By diving into your AOIs and following your curiosity, you've gathered a wealth of ingredients. General ingredients can be shelved in the vast pantry of your mind, while the more intriguing ones that are closer to forming solutions to existing problems or inventing new problems to solve should be placed in pots on your multi-burner stove, ready to simmer. The pots that require less attention—those needing more time to stew—should be moved to the back burners on a low simmer. Pots that are closer to achieving that perfect recipe and need more frequent monitoring should be shifted to the front burners, where the heat is higher. In this metaphor, simmering represents the process of allowing your life experiences and ideas to combine unconsciously and organically in your mind. It's arguably the most creative phase of the entire process and must be delicate, deliberate, and slow.

However, the simmering process in creativity isn't just about time. It's about giving ideas the space to breathe, grow, and find their own natural connections. Without air and space, ideas can become stifled, preventing the creative process from unfolding in ways that lead to fresh insights. However, despite its critical importance to innovation, *simmering remains the most overlooked part of the creative journey.*

In cooking, we let ingredients marinate, allowing them to rest and blend together. Similarly, in creativity, this phase of dormancy is like a stew simmering quietly on the stove—free from constant stirring or oversight. During this time, the flavors meld together and the essence of the problem or idea begins to emerge, much like a rich broth developing depth and complexity. Just as a well-simmered dish reveals its true flavors, this period of quiet reflection helps you deeply reconnect with the meat of your problem to solve.

How does the simmering process turn these disparate ingredients of life experience into creative solutions? Simmering is a method of cooking ingredients gently and slowly in liquid at a temperature just below boiling point. It's a very gentle process because the ingredients are protected by water that is maintained at a constant temperature so they cook extremely evenly. This allows the unique flavors of each ingredient to infuse their deliciousness into the liquid as they concentrate. Simmering is a beautiful process of give-and-take since the ingredients are not only contributing their unique flavors to the liquid but simultaneously absorbing a bit of that seasoned liquid, which creates a magical union. It's a perfect symbiosis in enhancing the flavor of every individual ingredient by allowing them all to simmer together and become tender. Also, through simmering, some of the liquid in the pot eventually evaporates, and by the time your recipe is ready to be served, the flavors will have become especially savory and intense.

When we neglect to simmer our ingredients and rush to a finish line with the first solution we conceive off the bat, we're combining those ingredients in the exact same way we have in the past. These solutions are retrieved entirely in the conscious mind without allowing the ingredients to recombine in any novel way. But when we allow simmering in the unconscious mind, there are no past recipes or formulaic patterns to turn to. Since we're not directing our ingredients toward a specific outcome and, instead, are allowing them to be entirely free from formal constraints, they are able to simmer and meld into a variety of new and unique combinations. By permitting this natural process, innovative and unconventional solutions, often disregarded by the conscious mind, can flourish and develop into feasible alternatives.[1]

The key elements of simmering include alternating between attending to the simmering pot and leaving it alone, controlling your simmer, allowing your simmering process to take as much time as necessary, and spending time away from your simmering process. Let's discuss these in further detail now.

ALTERNATING BETWEEN ATTENDING TO THE SIMMERING POT AND LEAVING IT ALONE

In the process of simmering, you need to alternate between periods of checking in on the ingredients in your pot and stirring them while also allowing them to simmer independently. This is the stage where you can taste the concoction and experiment with enhancing the recipe by incorporating additional ingredients from the pantry or tweaking the levels of ingredients already in the pot. You can also "spice it up" by introducing new seasonings to elevate the flavors, aiming for a harmonious blend where all elements come together in a truly extraordinary way.

Controlling Your Simmer

You have considerable control over how you simmer your ingredients, depending on their specific cooking requirements. This approach parallels the time and focus you dedicate to addressing your AOI or problem to solve. For example, a slow simmer might be needed when your ingredients require more time to blend fully or when the problem you're addressing is particularly complex. A slow simmer, set on low heat, involves minimal activity in the pot and requires less active attention, allowing the ingredients to meld quietly. A medium simmer, set on medium-low heat, produces a gentle bubbling and needs occasional checking but not intense engagement. This method is suitable for problems that are nearing resolution but still need a bit more time to come together. In contrast, a rapid simmer, set on medium to medium-high heat, is a more vigorous process and requires close monitoring, frequent stirring, and careful temperature adjustments to prevent boiling over. This approach is ideal for solutions that are nearly ready but need final refinements and enhancements before presentation.

Allowing Your Simmering Process to Take as Much Time as Necessary

A chef website discusses how to make a mirepoix (soup stock) from scratch.[2] It stresses the critical importance of not rushing the simmering process because boiling is too violent an action and will cause the stock to become cloudy. If soup bones and water are brought to a gentle simmer, it forces out the impurities, which thicken, group together, and ultimately rise to the top of the pot. Then the chef can skim them off the surface before they drop back down into the liquid. If this process happens too rapidly because of a vigorous boil, the impurities (also called scum—defined as extraneous matter formed on the surface of a liquid, often as a foul, filmy covering[3]) don't rise to the surface of the liquid in clusters and are instead brought back down into the stock before they are able to be skimmed off. This is considered tainted and faulty stock because it's filled with impurities and is cloudy versus crystal clear.

In fine restaurants, this faulty stock would be disposed of and never served. Think of your concepts in the same manner. You don't want to rush the process of bringing them to reality and poison them with contaminants that cloud their clarity and beauty. This only leads to substandard products and solutions—ones that no one wants or that fail to deliver real value.

Spending Time Away from Your Simmering Ingredients

Once the stove temperature is adjusted and all your ingredients are in the pot, put the cover on and let them simmer away. The capacity to stop "doing" and completely detach from the simmering problem after intense periods of concentration is essential for the arrival of inspiration. You cannot receive novel recipes from the subconscious mind if the conscious mind is continually consumed or exhausted. Inventive recipes need lots of freedom and space to cross from the unconscious to the conscious mind. In giving your ingredients/problem to solve time to independently simmer, you can choose to 1) consciously work on other problems, 2) engage in hobbies, or 3) refrain from conscious mental work altogether as your ingredients continue to bubble and simmer and the problem is pondered at a subconscious level.[4] Your ingredients will keep cooking away and creating richer combinations *even when your attention is directed elsewhere*. That's the remarkable power of your brain!

Just as you select the simmering method for your ingredients, the way you spend time away from the problem you're pondering depends on the nature of the issue you're addressing. Tackling more complex issues necessitates extended periods of downtime, during which the unconscious or partially conscious mind is free to engage in undisturbed, unrestricted processing. In these situations, your time spent away from the problem to solve should include truly mindful and relaxing activities that put your mind at complete ease. These activities may sometimes even provide clues to potential creative solutions, as something unrelated to your simmering recipe could spark a connection between your conscious and unconscious mind that leads to a revelation. The activities you select during the simmering process are very personal, and what works beautifully for one person may impact another negatively.[5]

A Taste of Practice

Your personal practice to maximize the potential of the simmering process may include:

- **ENGAGING IN ACTIVITIES THAT REQUIRE MINIMAL MENTAL EFFORT** and generate the right conditions and attitude that are conducive to contemplation. These include walking in natural beauty and natural light and engaging in other forms of movement like running, swimming, dancing, and bicycling. Taking baths or showers, gardening, cooking, driving, and crafting are also conducive to mindfulness. These activities must make your conscious mind free from interference and disturbances and uncluttered enough to allow new ideas to arise in the unconscious. The most enjoyable way I simmer ingredients is by walking along the shoreline collecting shells. Intently focusing my mind on finding that elusive gem is just the thing to help me subconsciously generate new ideas!

- **LISTENING TO CERTAIN TYPES OF MUSIC** that allow the mind to wander can also be conducive to daydreaming and conceiving novel solutions. I personally require uplifting music to enter a creative state and avoid tunes that evoke sadness or negative emotions. I also find that I can't listen to songs with familiar lyrics, as my mind gets too caught up in recalling the words and singing along, preventing me from fully freeing my thoughts to openly ideate. If a favorite song gets stuck on repeat in my brain, it obstructs the mental space needed for creative thinking. During brainstorming, it's crucial that the music remains in the background and doesn't draw your focus. That's why genres like jazz, piano, deep house, and uplifting instrumentals work best during the simmering process because they provide the mental air your brain needs, allowing ideas to flow and recombine effectively.

- **FREQUENTLY SWITCHING TASKS** to allow your mind to experience all sorts of different stimuli. Avoid falling into a routine and instead consistently explore new approaches that introduce fresh ideas and ingredients, creating more opportunities for alternative solutions.

- **ALLOWING YOUR MIND TO WANDER, FOLLOWING TOPICS OR IDEAS THAT PIQUE YOUR INTEREST** and always keeping a notepad or phone handy to capture interesting ideas or thoughts that arise. Creativity researcher R. E. M. Harding emphasized the transient nature of inspiring ideas and impressions—vivid and clear in the moment yet quickly fading if not recorded. She stated, "Inspiration does not continue long."[6] In fact, Tchaikovsky declared, "If that condition of mind and soul, which we call inspiration, lasted long without intermission, no artist could survive it. The strings would break and the instrument be shattered into fragments."[7]

- **EMBRACING THE BELIEF THAT THE ANSWERS ARE WITHIN YOU, WAITING TO EMERGE WITH TIME AND SPACE.** You must believe that with ample time and patience to allow your ingredients to simmer, a novel answer to every problem will emerge. A positive mindset is crucial for having confidence in your ability to create innovative solutions and for committing the time needed to allow your ideas to fully develop.

- **PRIMING YOUR MIND WITH INTERESTING IDEAS AND PERSPECTIVES OUTSIDE YOUR OWN.** For some problems, it's valuable to actively seek out other stimulating minds and engage in invigorating intellectual discussions while the problem is simmering. Talk about your topic with others who are passionate about it as well, explain to others what you are doing to better clarify your ideas, read articles, listen to podcasts, and attend lectures given on your topic! Also, seek out those who disagree with you and try to convince them of your views.

- **REVELING IN THE JOURNEY, INSTEAD OF THE OUTCOME,** and fighting against wanting to develop conclusions too early in the simmering process. The recipe needs to unfold in its own time with as little meddling as possible.[8]

It's also important to recognize that you will engage in the simmering process multiple times throughout the full process of bringing your recipe to fruition. In fact, whenever you encounter an impasse or creative block or receive critical feedback that triggers reactivity and needs time to digest, it's a signal to throw all the ingredients back into the pot and let them simmer a bit more, allowing new solutions and insights to develop into something truly refined and compelling.

A Full Serving of Practice

It's essential to explore which activities best support your personal creative process—those that allow you to effortlessly immerse and focus your attention. These activities enable your mind to shift away from the problem at hand, letting it simmer away in the subconscious.

You may need to experiment with a variety of activities until you find the one that naturally helps your mind settle into a simmering state.

The most effective activity should vary depending on the nature of the problem you are trying to solve. In my experience, more complex problems require activities that minimally and gently captivate my attention, remaining in the background of my mind while my simmering ingredients have enough freedom and room in the forefront to recombine. For less challenging problems that require less mental effort to solve, I can give more focused attention to the activity itself, which can stimulate my mind more intensely.

Despite the type of problem you're tackling, one activity that's commonly effective for sparking insight is walking in nature. However, what you engage with during that walk is important. For example, keeping your mind too focused and active can prevent it from wandering and may block inspiration from flowing. If I'm trying to solve a complex problem, I avoid information-heavy podcasts or anything that clutters my mind or makes me overthink. I must resist the urge to cram more facts into my already-overflowing brain and allow the existing information to blend and recombine organically.

One common practice I find particularly helpful is the 5-4-3-2-1 mindfulness technique developed by Dr. Ellen Hendricksen, a clinical psychologist for the Center for Anxiety & Related Disorders at Boston University. I focus on five things I can see, four things I can hear, three things I can smell, two things I can touch, and one thing I can taste. This sensory practice, especially when done in nature, immerses you in the extraordinary wonder of the present moment while letting your ingredients gently simmer below the surface. Over time, you'll discover which activities are most effective, as profound revelations and creative insights often arise during or right after those that resonate most and help you enter flow state!

Chew on This . . .

Try this **Savor the Spark** exercise to ground you in the present moment and give creative thoughts space to simmer and meld naturally.

- **BEGIN WITH A QUICK STIR:** Ask a simple question to guide your thoughts:

  - What's something I'm curious about today?
  - What's one word or image that inspires me right now?
  - What's one thing I've recently noticed that I didn't before?

- **FIRE UP YOUR SPARK:** Choose a brief activity that ignites your creativity while still allowing room for mind-wandering. Examples include:

  - Write one sentence or draw a simple image inspired by the prompt.
  - Rearrange items in your desk or closet into a new layout or interesting pattern.
  - Take a short walk and notice three surprising details around you (e.g., colors, smells, people, or sounds).
  - Hum or tap out a familiar tune.

- **SEASON THE INSIGHT:** Allow a moment to reflect on the activity. Ask yourself the following questions, then take one slow, deep breath to savor your sense of curiosity and appreciation:

    - What surprised or fascinated me during this exercise?
    - Did any unusual insights arise?
    - How might this insight impact my thinking or recipe?

THE REASONS WE MAY BE TEMPTED TO BYPASS THE SIMMERING PROCESS

Many entrepreneurs bypass the step of simmering and rush to serve a finished recipe, even though the process is so critical to creating groundbreaking recipes. This tendency can stem from various factors, including misconceptions about productivity or a fixation on one enticing idea.

Belief That Simmering Equals Laziness

Many of us are conditioned by society to believe that any period of inaction equates to being "lazy" or a "slacker." Because of this belief, when we allow ourselves the time to step back and let our ideas simmer and marinate, we often feel guilty, as though we're shirking our responsibility to be efficient and productive and churn out a continual stream of content.

I was recently speaking with a friend who shared that she'd been feeling overwhelmed with guilt for procrastinating on her work and not being more motivated. I was surprised because she was the *last* person I would ever call a slacker. She explained that she was currently working on two books and several articles simultaneously.

But she was also passionate about gardening, and in between writing, she often found herself pausing to tend to the many specimen plants in her office. Sometimes, she'd spend hours on this seemingly unrelated task in the middle of the day. She was frustrated that she kept feeling this powerful urge to step away from her projects and engage in what she saw as a frivolous activity.

I asked her what happened after she finished her gardening, and she told me she always returned to work refreshed and ready to dive into hours of focused, productive, and inspired writing. I had to smile because this brilliant woman had no idea that she wasn't being lazy at all! The truth was that her time spent away from her deadlines was essential to the creative process, as she was unconsciously allowing her ideas to simmer and recombine into new insights. In fact, she was doing *exactly* what was required for her true creativity to flourish!

Once my friend realized that she wasn't shirking her responsibilities by allowing her ideas to simmer, a huge weight of shame and guilt was lifted off her shoulders. This newfound freedom allowed her to embrace the full creative process, tapping into her capacity to innovate organically without pressure to continually produce! She recognized that those moments of pause were an essential part of her natural flow, helping her innovate more effectively. Embracing the concept of simmering may likewise allow you to view downtime, hobbies, and periods of reflection not as trivial distractions but as essential elements of the process of conceiving innovative ideas!

However, what if the reason you're having trouble being productive isn't because your creative ingredients need more time to simmer but because your brain is wired differently? If you have ADHD, your struggles with focus or motivation may not be about laziness, procrastination, or allowing time for simmering but rather may stem from the unique way your brain processes tasks. People with ADHD often experience difficulty in maintaining sustained attention on one topic, which can make it feel impossible to settle into a deep flow of work. This doesn't mean you're incapable of being productive; it just means that the typical advice about long, uninterrupted, focused work bursts may not apply to you. In fact, those with differently wired brains might find that their best work happens in shorter bursts of intense focus or after they've taken breaks to engage in something else—like walking, listening to music, or engaging in a mindful activity like doodling. The neurodivergent brain doesn't need to "wait" for inspiration to strike; instead, it thrives on shifting between tasks and coming back to things after a reset. Embracing this way of working, rather than pushing against it, can help you achieve true productivity and creativity without the guilt or frustration of trying to fit into conventional productivity norms.

Becoming Completely and Utterly Obsessed with Just One Idea

If you become too enamored with your initial idea, you may forge ahead to a finished product and bypass the simmering process necessary to assess its viability. Conviction in your ideas is extremely dangerous, not only because it makes you vulnerable to believing false positives but also because it impedes you from allowing the necessary time to generate a variety of alternative solutions. Without this flexibility, you risk creating products or services that don't truly solve a need. Instead, you end up with something that's either a rehash of what already exists or a wacky idea that no one wants or needs!

Getting to the right solution requires allowing your ingredients to properly simmer so you can generate the most inventive array of possibilities. If you cling too tightly to your preconceived notion of how the product or service should perform, without giving your unconscious mind the time it needs to refine the idea, the finished concept may end up lackluster and not adequately solve the real problems of its target market.

Having Conviction in Your Idea and Confirmation Bias

Once you develop a strong belief in your idea, you may also develop confirmation bias. "Confirmation bias" is a psychological term coined by English psychologist Peter Wason that describes the human tendency to only seek out information that confirms or strengthens a belief, position, expectation, or idea and to discount, ignore, or discredit information that doesn't support it. This causes you to have a bias toward your original position because if you only seek out information that supports your views, you will only find information that supports them. Instead of conducting thorough research and examining all evidence, you limit yourself to ideas that align with your preconceptions.[9] And once confirmation bias takes hold, it becomes challenging to overcome.

Story Nugget

I often encounter confirmation bias when mentoring entrepreneurs, as many of them erroneously believe that 1) their deeply personal problem is universal and their solution will naturally resonate with others and/or 2) their product is unique enough to cut through the clutter and achieve mass-market success.

Over the years, I've mentored multiple entrepreneurs who were late to address problems that were already well-covered by existing solutions, such as healthy vegan desserts and hypoallergenic skin-care products. While these were both legitimate needs, the proposed solutions struggled to gain traction in an already-saturated market. Both the healthy dessert and hypoallergenic skin-care sectors were highly competitive, with numerous established products already addressing those needs.

None of these new offerings were particularly differentiated or innovative, although one common claim among these entrepreneurs was that their products were "more natural" than existing options. However, despite their emphasis on ingredients, the market didn't seem to prioritize this factor. Glowing reviews and positive customer feedback indicated that consumers were overwhelmingly satisfied with the current offerings, suggesting that "ultranatural" wasn't a decisive differentiator.

These entrepreneurs overlooked clear data showing that consumers weren't concerned about the ingredients in existing options or seeking alternatives. They were so convinced that their solutions were perfect that they skipped the crucial steps of gathering relevant ingredients, exploring their AOI to better understand its nuances, and allowing the simmering process to unfold. By bypassing these stages, they missed key insights that would have revealed themselves with deeper market investigation and idea development. This lack of due diligence often leads to products that are either indistinguishable from what already exists or so personalized that they fail to resonate with a broader audience.

I gently reminded these entrepreneurs that while their ingredients may have been healthier and more natural, this alone wasn't enough to set their product apart. Yet their conviction in their solutions prevented them from fully exploring the market, hindering their ability to generate the fresh insights and ideas needed for success.

Stifling Creativity Through Developing Assumptions, Premature Conclusions, and Biases

Humans tend to rush to generalities based on preconceived notions and accept existing models and paradigms rather than start from scratch and look at problems at face value. Early on, your thoughts shouldn't even be focused on a specific solution or answer. Jumping to conclusions prevents you from truly understanding the problem, considering critical factors that impact the problem, and letting the ingredients simmer until you organically conceive innovative solutions. This results in repetitive, copycat solutions that struggle to compete with established brands in the market. You will be simply putting forth mundane solutions that do not improve or change a market and do not become a product or service that sells like hotcakes. This is because starting with a narrow focus, instead of initially gaining a broader vision and global perspective, limits your recipes to what have already been served.

Once you put in tremendous effort, become a bona fide expert in your AOI, and allow all those ingredients to simmer in the unconscious, you will interpret the area differently and see it from a completely unique perspective. This will allow you to better visualize the gaps and problems in what already exists, analyze where you fit, understand the limitations of your contributions, and learn where to invest your efforts.

A broader focus enables you to think more strategically, control the overall course of your actions, and gain the capacity to think ahead and plan. When you neglect to simmer your ingredients, you miss the relationships between them and the anomalies that hold the key to novel solutions. To understand problems completely, it's critical to distill them down to their individual ingredients, throw them all into the pot, and believe "I won't know the answer until they have a chance to simmer together and give me the answer!" Humans make assumptions and jump to conclusions because they fear the unknown and new ideas.

The unknown makes us uncomfortable and scared, which can trigger a fight-or-flight response. So we unconsciously make assumptions, jump to conclusions, and follow our preconceived notions about the way things "should be." Our unhealthy egos would rather feel certain, react swiftly, and make rash decisions than examine the data objectively and let it lead us to the answer. We get so stuck in what we already know that we don't have the courage to say, "I don't know if others will like this, and I need more information until I know!" If you want to create something truly revolutionary, treat the immediate solutions that come to mind as additional ingredients to toss into the already-simmering pot and keep starting from scratch, allowing the process to naturally unfold.

Fearing and resisting new ideas is called herd mentality, which encourages us to conform to societal standards and oppose any deviation from convention.[10] Additionally, many adults succumb to the attack-escape reaction. When they first become conscious of something new, they usually either attack or try to escape from it. Criticism can take mild forms, such as ridicule, while avoidance may simply involve ignoring the new idea altogether.[11] These responses are often accompanied by rationalizations, where the critic provides reasons for their rejection. Skepticism frequently arises as a natural defense mechanism against unfamiliar ideas. How frequently do we find ourselves instinctively pushing back against new concepts presented to us before we fully contemplate them? As physicist Alan Walsh says, "The itch to suffocate the infant idea burns in all of us."[12]

Story Nugget

> One of our categories at M&D was a line of adorable, full-body hand puppets. They could only be merchandised on large wire spinner racks, requiring three square feet of precious retail

Melissa & Doug full-body hand puppets (original design), bulky and requiring a freestanding spinner rack, were discontinued due to poor sales.

Melissa & Doug themed hand puppets (new design), sold in four-puppet sets for easy wall display, became bestsellers.

space. While children loved playing with these puppets, they didn't perform well enough to justify that level of space allocation in our retailers. Based on consistent sales data, our team ultimately jumped to the conclusion that the puppet category was weak and should be discontinued.

Puppets were a beloved classic, and I believed the poor sales were due not to a lack of popularity but rather to their merchandising challenges. I wasn't yet ready to abandon the category altogether. To solve the space challenge, I created sets of four themed hand puppets that retailed for under $20, could be easily pegged on store slatwalls, and didn't require a freestanding fixture. These new sets performed so well that we ended up creating an entire category of hand-puppet sets. This experience proved once again that it's always critical to look below surface-level data to fully understand what's truly happening. Only then can we create an effective solution that sells like hotcakes!

A Taste of Practice

Your personal practice to facilitate the simmering process may include:

- **CULTIVATING PATIENCE** in realizing that innovation is an ongoing process requiring time and persistence. Give yourself permission to let ideas develop naturally rather than holding to a strict deadline and forcing quick solutions. Keep reminding yourself that significant breakthroughs cannot be rushed and often take decades.

- **EMBRACING THE PROCESS OF EXPLORATION** and exploring different angles, perspectives, and approaches over attaining immediate results. Allow your mind to wander and consider a variety of possibilities without immediately trying to solve the problem. This will help you shift your focus from the result to the journey of discovery. Embrace the process as the goal and an opportunity for growth and learning.

- **DISCOVERING TRUE PASSIONS** through finding pastimes and hobbies that bring you so much joy that you're eager to let your ingredients simmer so you can engage in them! I have so many activities I love to pursue that I'm eager to push my ideas into the subconscious and let them evolve while I immerse myself in fun pursuits! Becoming engrossed in enjoyable activities that stimulate creativity and relaxation helps you embrace the simmering process, allowing ideas to develop organically. And now knowing that these activities serve a deeper purpose lets you enjoy them completely guilt-free!

- **PRIORITIZING REFLECTION TIME AND DOWNTIME** by allowing yourself breaks, even if you need to schedule them in your calendar. The practice of regularly stepping away from your recipe for quiet contemplation or brainstorming without interruptions can lead to breakthroughs when you return with a fresh perspective. Embracing this habit will not only enable the simmering process to ensue much more naturally but release any self-blame for taking frequent breaks!

- **SEEKING DIVERSE INPUT** by engaging in collaborative discussions with peers or mentors from various backgrounds and fields to gain feedback, new insights, and inspiration. Different perspectives can enrich the simmering process by helping ideas mature, take new directions, and lead to more innovative solutions.

- **ITERATING GRADUALLY AND FOCUSING ON THE LONG TERM** by working on your idea in incremental steps. Test and refine your concept gradually over time rather than aiming for immediate perfection. Focusing on long-term objectives and milestones rather than immediate results can reduce urgency, help maintain perspective, and encourage a more thoughtful and deliberate approach. Remember to celebrate incremental achievements and maintain your momentum without the pressure of a fixed deadline.

- **DOCUMENTING INSIGHTS** by keeping a journal or notes on spontaneous ideas, thoughts, and reflections. Reviewing these periodically can offer new ingredients of insight, provide new angles, and deepen your understanding of the problem over the long term.

- **CONTINUING TO LEARN** by engaging in ongoing education and skill development. New knowledge can provide additional ingredients to add to your simmering recipes, spark innovative ideas, and provide fresh perspectives that contribute to a successful simmering process.

A Full Serving of Practice

It's one thing to be patient enough to allow your ideas to simmer when there's no pressure of a looming deadline; it's another entirely when your creativity is required to hit a fixed schedule. If your livelihood involves a pipeline of creativity, there will be tension between needing to let your ideas evolve and the urgency of a deadline that demands results. On a human level, it's incredibly frustrating to prioritize the slow, organic process of idea development when you're expected to deliver results within a specific time frame.

However, this difficulty doesn't mean you should discard the concept of simmering altogether. Even within the constraints of a schedule, it's still possible and crucial to give your ideas the space they need to naturally develop and simmer to perfection. The key is learning how to allow that simmering to unfold without losing sight of the deadline.

How can we best allow simmering to happen on a timeline? Some of my strategies include:

- **CARVING OUT PERIODS OF TIME** and allowing space for unconscious brainstorming and quiet reflection, even while the clock is ticking. This may include sitting quietly and letting your wind wander, taking a brief walk around the block, or listening to music.

- **ALLOWING YOUR SUBCONSCIOUS MIND TO KEEP EVOLVING THOSE IDEAS** throughout each day. Intentionally visualize dropping your problem to solve into the subconscious. Then just let it continue to simmer below the surface during your periods of downtime.

- **BREAKING YOUR PROBLEM INTO STAGES AND ALLOWING FOR ITERATIVE PROGRESS** rather than waiting for the big idea to emerge before moving forward. For example, with a consumer product, you can focus on the materials you'll use or the color palette. This enables you to move forward with the project while still refining your ideas along the way by allowing all those small insights to still simmer as the larger ones emerge.

- **RESISTING FORCING OUT A STREAM OF MEDIOCRE IDEAS** by trusting in the process. Even if you need to cut the process short before solutions emerge, it is still better to let ideas unfold in their own time. This will ultimately set the stage for breakthroughs later in the process, even if they emerge down the road!

- **SETTING CLEAR CHECKPOINTS** that enable you to assess the state of your ideas and know when it is time to move from simmering to execution.

- **PRACTICING BALANCING THE PATIENCE ESSENTIAL FOR SIMMERING WITH THE ACTION NEEDED TO MEET**

DEADLINES. If you can learn to work with the simmering process rather than against it, allowing the process to unfold while also taking productive steps as you go, it will inspire the final outcome.

Chew on This . . .

Try this daily **Simmer Support** exercise to shift pressure to possibility, fostering organic idea development within the constraints of deadlines and fixed schedules.

- **SELECT YOUR KEY INGREDIENT:** Identify one urgent problem to solve or question to answer that has a deadline. State it aloud, and agree to simply let it *simmer* rather than racing to formulate immediate solutions.

- **SCHEDULE SIMMER SESSIONS:** Schedule one or two simmer sessions into your day. These can include stretching, relaxing silently in a comfortable position, listening to music, or taking a brief walk. As you engage in these activities, visualize the challenge in the top of your mind slowly slipping into the subconscious. Allow your thoughts to flow naturally without judgment as you surrender the need for immediate answers.

- **SPICE UP YOUR DAYDREAMING:** Brainstorm alternative answers to your problem/question without pressuring yourself to devise concrete solutions. If it makes it easier, break your problem into smaller, actionable components and focus on one piece during your simmer sessions rather than worrying about the larger idea.

- **TASTE-TEST BREAKTHROUGHS:** Capture any fleeting thoughts or minor insights that you've cooked up, even if they are not yet fully formed. These little breakthroughs may feed your larger ideas down the road. However, the key is never to force a perfect solution but rather to record whatever naturally emerges.

- **SEASON TO TASTE:** Reflect on today's practice, note any ideas or insights that arose during your sessions, and assess your progress on smaller tasks. Then adjust tomorrow's simmer and work balance, if necessary.

cherry on top
SIMMERING YOUR SECRET SAUCE

You should never begin any form of concept-building work until you have given the simmering process ample time to allow the ingredients to meld and recombine in innovative ways. This stage is crucial, as it provides the mental space for your ideas to organically evolve, unlocking their full potential. By engaging in the process of simmering, you create the conditions for your ideas to transform into something truly extraordinary rather than rushing and forcing them into the world prematurely.

4

YOUR RECIPE IS READY

Unveiling the Solution to Your Problem

After ample simmering, your chef's-kiss recipe (the solution to your existing problem to solve or a fresh concept altogether) may appear in a streak of illumination seemingly out of nowhere. It might seem like a sudden burst of brilliance, but it's actually the result of leisurely ingredient gathering and patient cooking. Just as a well-developed sauce can surprise with its depth and richness, your solution can emerge with clarity and insight, even if it appears to come out of the blue.

However, neither tantalizing recipes nor knowledge acquisition arise instantaneously without any prior preparation, information, or elaboration. Sometimes we may be unaware of the catalyst or event that existed before the aha moment and insight-generation stage, so we may believe that the new knowledge wasn't prepared in advance. But it isn't magic; it's your *intuition* that has been sparked during the simmering process. Totally and consciously immersing yourself in the problem or an AOI so your mind is completely engorged with its ingredients (facts/information) is the most important prerequisite for developing intuition. The conscious mind must contemplate the problem for an extended period and become completely immersed in its ingredients to spark the subconscious mind to begin the simmering process. The more pertinent ingredients (facts/information) the mind has available to use, the higher the likelihood that the simmering process will produce a chef's-kiss recipe from those ingredients and conceive one or more solutions to the problem or a completely novel concept.[1]

Individuals who deeply immerse themselves in an AOI for many years develop extensive memory networks and pathways in their brains. These networks constantly seek and find connections among various pieces of information as the expert develops a keen sense of how different elements interact. When faced with a problem, the search branches out in numerous directions below the level of conscious awareness, activating various networks. Experts guided by an instinctive sense of correctness can develop and intuit patterns or solutions instantaneously. Solutions suddenly emerge into consciousness and become firmly embedded in memory. Over time, all these memories merge into a dynamic pattern, forming what is known as "consolidated" long-term memories in our synapses. Intuitions initially start faint but strengthen with experience, as experts can summon more intuitions and integrate them more deeply with their rational thought processes. The process of developing intuition is purely a result of investing time and cannot be simplified.[2]

THE IMPORTANCE OF CULTIVATING EMPATHY

To create products and services that serve all types of individuals, you need to be able to see them clearly and experience what they experience in every sense. A lack of empathy will have you seeing others through your distorted biases, making you critical and judgmental, which is not conducive to creativity. You'll need to develop a high level of compassionate empathy, which combines cognitive empathy—the ability to understand another person's thoughts and perspectives—with affective empathy—the ability to understand another person's emotions.[3] Only through developing empathy can you actively participate in others' realities and create products and services that *truly serve their needs*.

The more you can build your capacity for empathy, the more you can develop products intuitively by deepening your sensitivity to emotional cues, enriching your understanding of human emotions, and improving your ability to recognize behavioral patterns. Empathy sharpens your intuitive skills by helping you closely engage with others' feelings and interpret their body language, allowing you to better anticipate and respond to their needs and emotions. Additionally, the self-awareness gained through empathetic interactions helps clarify and refine your intuitive insights.

Empathy enhances intuition by increasing sensitivity to emotional cues, which allows you to detect subtle signals and patterns in others' feelings and reactions. This deeper emotional understanding enriches your ability to anticipate how people might respond in various situations. As you recognize patterns in behaviors and emotions over time, your intuition sharpens, helping you predict outcomes more accurately.

Empathy also improves your nonverbal communication skills, making you adept at reading body language and facial expressions, further refining your ability to gauge others' needs and emotions. Additionally, the strong emotional connections built through empathy foster trust and openness, offering more nuanced insights. Finally, practicing empathy encourages self-awareness, helping you differentiate between your emotions and those of others, which enhances the clarity and accuracy of your intuitive insights. In essence, empathy is a bridge connecting you more deeply to others while also strengthening your understanding of yourself.

A Taste of Practice

Your practice for developing enhanced empathy may include:

- **LISTENING CLOSELY** to what others say without interruption. Reflect on their feelings and perspectives to better understand their experience.

- **SEEING SITUATIONS FROM OTHER PEOPLE'S PERSPECTIVE.** Imagine how you would feel if you were in their position.

- **ENGAGING WITH DIVERSE PERSPECTIVES,** including different cultures, experiences, and backgrounds. Reading books, watching films, or engaging in conversations with people from various backgrounds can help broaden your understanding.

- **PRACTICING COMPASSION** and showing kindness and understanding toward others. Engage in small acts of kindness to foster empathy and create connections.

- **ASKING QUESTIONS** to better understand someone's honest feelings and experiences. This shows genuine interest and helps you learn more about their perspective.

- **REFLECTING ON YOUR OWN EMOTIONS** and understanding how your feelings and reactions are universal to all humans. This self-awareness can help you better relate to others' emotions.

- **PRACTICING MINDFULNESS** to enable yourself to be more present and aware of your interactions. This can help you tune into the emotions and needs of others more effectively.

By consistently applying these practices, you can deepen your empathy, strengthen your relationships, and develop products that more effectively meet others' needs.

A Full Serving of Practice

One of the ways to develop empathy is to understand the perspectives of others who hold views that are completely different from our own. This is not simply about hearing their words or reading about their views; it's about diving deeper into the why behind their beliefs, actions, choices, and decisions.

A practical way to put this into action is by looking at a situation like an election, where opposing sides seem to be at odds with each other on nearly every issue. To truly understand the other side, we must understand what drives them, looking at their dreams, desires, fears, and motivations. We must realize that an individual's choices are deeply influenced by their life experience and core beliefs. When we understand those values, we gain insight into the person behind the vote, and our empathy for them grows.

It's only once we understand another's fears and hopes that we can truly begin to feel what they feel and see the world through their eyes. Then, even if we disagree with them, we can still understand where their decisions come from and empathize with the values and intentions that shaped their choices. We can connect with them on a human level and gain insight into their hearts and minds, even if we think differently. Once we have sought to understand, listen, and communicate with others, we'll be more compassionate in our engagements, more open in our conversations, and more empathetic regarding others' motivations.

Chew on This . . .

Try this **Taste the World Through Their Palate** exercise to foster deeper empathy by exploring the unique flavors of someone else's perspective.

- **CHOOSE A NEW FLAVOR:** Choose a person you disagree with or whose choices, behaviors, or beliefs you find puzzling. It could be a family member, a public figure, or even a character in a book or news story.

- **SAMPLE THEIR DISH:** Pretend you are living their life and ask yourself:

  - What life experiences or fears might have led them to think this way?

  - What is most important to them, and what do they value most deeply?

  - What does the world look like from their perspective?

- **FIND THE COMMON INGREDIENT:** Identify one thing you have in common with this individual, even if your views differ. It could be a shared dream, hope, or fear.

- **SHARE THE INGREDIENT:** Voice an insight you gained from this exercise. For example, you could say, "Their perspective is based on a need to belong to their community, and even though I view the issue differently, I now better understand it."

- **BLEND IT INTO YOUR RECIPE:** Carry the new insight into your life, and whenever you encounter differing perspectives, remember this exercise and strive to listen and respond with empathy.

TRUSTING THE SIMMERING PROCESS TO HONOR YOUR INTUITION

It has taken me decades to honor and completely trust my intuition. I now recognize that even as a child, I experienced those "sparks of knowing" that we all encounter from time to time. However, I was so focused on seeking external validation and worrying about others' opinions that I ignored those gut instincts, instead following what I thought would please others or heeding the advice of those I believed to be more experienced. I mistakenly thought that others must be wiser and that my own gut reactions would never measure up. Over time, I learned that knowledge is power. By building a solid foundation of expertise in my AOI, I became best equipped to make decisions for my business and life more generally. While this didn't guarantee that every decision was perfect, having the freshest and most relevant ingredients meant my choices were the best possible guides at the time.

Every day, I'm approached with challenging questions from individuals who expect immediate answers. My history as a people pleaser often drives me to offer quick, surface-level responses that are designed to appease them and showcase my ability to provide instant solutions. However, I've come to realize that this approach does a disservice to both them and me. These quick answers usually lack depth and consideration, failing to truly address the question at hand. It took considerable courage for me to respond by saying, "That's a tough question. I need some time to think it over and will get back to you." Initially, this pause was met with annoyance by those accustomed to immediate answers and instant gratification. Yet I now understand that taking the time to deliver well-considered, thoughtful responses is not only better for others but also aligns with my commitment to authenticity and excellence.

When faced with difficult decisions, our instinct is often to panic. We might feel our heart race, our breathing become shallow, a flush creep over us, and our blood pressure rise. This heightened state can easily trigger a fight/flight/freeze response, which causes us to attack the question itself, freeze and not give any answer, or rattle off a stream of reactive, knee-jerk answers. Instead of succumbing to these states, I practice staying calm and adopting a Start-from-Scratch mentality.

I take a moment to calmly frame the challenging question, say it aloud, and let it settle into my subconscious, where it can simmer alongside the various insights I've gathered from my life experiences. Sometimes my ingredients swiftly recombine and the solution presents itself in an immediate flash of clarity. Other times, the answer takes days, weeks, or even months to emerge. I've learned not to rush this process; if an answer doesn't arise organically, it means I might still be missing key ingredients or need more simmering time for solutions or ideas to fully develop. Trusting in this process has been transformative. It has relieved me from the pressure of fabricating answers that don't truly reflect who I am. I've gained the strength to admit "I don't know yet" while committing to finding the answer in a way that feels most authentic to me.

I must reiterate that, despite these intuitive flashes of insight, intuition is by no means guaranteed to be correct. It reflects your instinctive understanding at that moment, but that doesn't mean it will necessarily lead to winning ideas. This occurs because intuition stems from the imperfect human mind, and therefore, it might later be proven incorrect and easily fade from memory. *Intuitive* is simply an adjective that describes the way by which we arrive at a conclusion, but it has no bearing on the caliber of the idea itself. We must subject our intuitive ideas to the assessment process to determine if they are products and services that have the potential to sell like hotcakes. However, despite their frequent fallibility, developing a strong intuition to guide you from within is a key element of cooking up revolutionary ideas.

IN THE ABSENCE OF INTUITION

What if an epiphany doesn't arise after letting your ingredients simmer for an ample amount of time? If a clear solution or answer doesn't present itself after an extensive period of simmering, *it's simply not yet ready to arise*. This is no cause for alarm. It's merely indicating that your recipe may need additional ingredients, different proportions of ingredients, or more time to simmer. Alternatively, it could mean that the recipe in that pot may never be viable. Or perhaps it's simply ahead of its time, although you won't recognize that in the moment. The key is to keep engaging in life experiences, gathering more ingredients, and bringing new aspects of yourself to the AOI or problem to solve. Try not to rush the process, as that is the enemy of creativity. It's the process itself, not the goal, that matters, and many epiphanies aren't ready to surface until much later in life.

However, there will be many instances when you are forced to make an immediate decision and cannot wait for your intuition to speak. In such cases, use every relevant ingredient you have at that moment to make the best decision possible. The decision you make may not ultimately be the best one due to missing ingredients, but as you move forward and gather more relevant ones, you'll be better equipped to make more informed choices at future crossroads.

Story Nugget

I fell prey to one of the two main obstacles to creativity when writing the outline for this book: the pressure to meet a deadline and the desire to be seen as a star pupil. I took my decades of notes, insights, and experiences and raced to mold them into a compelling format. But as the deadline approached, I was still disappointed with my product. It didn't feel at all innovative or groundbreaking and more a replication of what already existed. I felt frustrated and anxious because despite knowing I had a unique perspective on creative entrepreneurship, I was struggling to uncover it among the hundreds of pages of notes and decades of accumulated experience. I just couldn't seem to rise above my ingredients to derive my unique perspective. As I pondered why I was unable to find my unique voice among others' research, I had a monumental epiphany: *I had neglected to let my ingredients go through the simmering process!*

I was dumbfounded that my goal of meeting a deadline had caused me to make the very same mistake I was cautioning others against! I then had no choice but to apologetically tell my editor that I was going to be late with my outline. I couldn't even tell her how late because I didn't know how long the simmering process would take. I then threw every single ingredient into a huge pot on a slow simmer, tightly affixed the lid, and put it on a back burner in my mind. I then put the outline *completely* out of my mind, engaging in activities I hadn't enjoyed in months, like listening to music, ideating other products, walking on the beach, crafting, and catching up with friends.

My simmering process took exactly *four full days*. On the fifth day, I was driving home along the highway, and BAM, I was suddenly bowled over by my utterly original, intuitive take on creativity. And it was *nothing* like the story I had been weaving the prior week. I was so overwhelmed by that pristine, authentic recipe that I needed to pull my car over and sob with relief and joy. I now knew, with every ounce of my being, that it was finally "Melissa's original recipe." I was then able to swiftly rewrite the outline, which is the format of the book you are now reading. I'm still amazed that I somehow skipped the simmering process, as it's the most crucial step in creating an authentic recipe!

Albert Einstein championed the value of allowing ideas to marinate over time. The journey from his initial insights to the publication of his groundbreaking theories of relativity spanned roughly a decade. As he humbly noted, "It's not that I'm so smart; it's just that I stay with problems longer."[4] This reflected his belief in the power of perseverance and the simmering process—where deep and sustained reflection leads to profound discoveries.

THE CONSEQUENCES OF DENYING INTUITION

Our hesitation to trust our intuition and the fear of making challenging decisions often leads us to intentionally narrow down our options. While this approach simplifies the decision-making process by offering only a few choices, it can also constrain potential solutions, resulting in more conventional outcomes and stifling innovation. By limiting our options, we risk missing out on unique and creative possibilities that could drive more groundbreaking and effective solutions. While some may prefer fewer choices to reduce anxiety—a sentiment echoed by Søren Kierkegaard's notion that "anxiety is the dizziness of freedom"—true innovators thrive on having a full buffet of options.[5] This expansive approach fosters the most inventive combinations and novel outcomes.

Story Nugget

> Our Lifelines engineers recently presented me with three options for the size of a new diffuser: small, medium, and large. This approach confined me to choose among only these three sizes despite the possibility of sizes outside this range or in between the provided options. This constraint not only limited my choice in size but also focused my attention solely on these predefined options, neglecting to ask anything about the aesthetic appeal of the *design itself*. For the first time in my career, I recognized this narrowing and marveled at how often we intentionally restrict our choices too early in the creative process.

Lifelines Cloud Diffuser (first prototype).

Recognizing this bias, I relied on my intuition to review the entire product as a whole and guide me toward a more aesthetically pleasing solution. Realizing that I didn't entirely love the design itself, I enhanced it by raising its base and changing the shape of the lid for greater height and presence. Then, I chose a size that fell between two of the original options. This intuitive decision-making process highlighted how

Lifelines Cloud Diffuser (final production design).

prematurely narrowing options can stifle creativity and limit the potential of the final product. Allowing a broader range of possibilities and trusting my instincts ultimately led to a more refined and impactful design, demonstrating the importance of keeping an open mind and leveraging intuitive insights in decision-making.

A Taste of Practice

Your personal practice for honing a powerful sense of intuition may include:

- **PRACTICING MINDFULNESS** by focusing on the here and now to help you become more aware of your thoughts, feelings, and bodily sensations and better able to tune into your intuitive insights.

- **LISTENING TO YOUR GUT FEELINGS** by paying attention to your immediate, intuitive reactions or feelings about situations. This can offer you valuable guidance, as these instincts are based on subconscious processing.

- **REFLECTING ON PAST EXPERIENCES** where your intuition guided you well or where you ignored it can help you understand patterns and better recognize and trust your intuition in the future.

- **REDUCING STRESS** through relaxation techniques, exercise, or hobbies since high stress can cloud your judgment and make it harder to access intuitive insights.

- **CULTIVATING SELF-AWARENESS** by dedicating time to assessing your personal values, beliefs, and emotions since greater self-awareness can help you better understand the source and validity of your intuitive feelings.

- **ENGAGING IN CREATIVE ACTIVITIES** that stimulate creativity and enhance your ability to tap into intuitive insights, such as gardening, drawing, or listening to or playing music.

- **KEEPING A JOURNAL** to record your intuitive thoughts, feelings, and experiences will allow you to notice patterns or recurring themes over time that can help you better understand and trust your intuition.

- **SEEKING SOLITUDE** and being alone with your thoughts will help you better hear and trust your intuitive voice without external distractions. Solitude is an essential element of self-discovery, giving you the space to become familiar with your mind. Therefore, it's important to allocate time for solitude and quiet reflection.

- **LEARNING FROM OTHERS** by observing and seeking advice from individuals who have strong intuitive abilities will help you absorb their strategies on how to tap into and utilize your own internal compass.

- **PRACTICING DECISION-MAKING** by regularly making decisions based on your intuition can help you develop and refine your intuitive skills over time.

- **ASKING OPEN-ENDED QUESTIONS** when faced with decisions will help you explore your feelings and thoughts more deeply, ultimately uncovering intuitive insights that might not be immediately obvious.

- **TRUSTING YOUR INSTINCTS** and building confidence in your intuition by starting with small decisions and gradually applying them to more significant choices. As you see positive outcomes, your trust in your intuition will grow.

A Full Serving of Practice

As a people pleaser, I became incredibly skilled at making decisions that would win the approval of others. I always ignored my gut instincts in favor of seeking validation from my peers and family. In fact, when I was ten years old, despite being creative and far from rigid, I decided I wanted to become a lawyer—simply because I thought it would make people say, "Wow, that's amazing" when I told them.

It wasn't until adulthood, when I met Doug, that I was asked what *I* wanted for the very first time. That question triggered an all-out panic attack because I had no idea what he wanted me to say—or even what I truly wanted. Learning what I felt, needed, and believed became a decades-long journey of self-discovery. Instead of looking to others for answers, I had to look inward and figure out what truly made me tick. At first, this was terrifying because I was so afraid of being judged or questioned. But over time, I learned to embrace my preferences, my opinions, my unique style, and my perspective on the world. To my surprise, I realized I was incredibly dogmatic and firm in my beliefs. For decades, I had been deferring to others, but the truth was I was a lioness—fierce, assertive, and unapologetic.

As my confidence grew, so did my intuition. I began trusting my inner knowing and found that answers and ideas would emerge from that blank canvas of imagination. I also came to understand that developing intuition requires patience through the process of simmering. I learned that if I rushed to make decisions to meet a deadline or avoid displeasing others, I would inevitably regret my poor choices and admonish myself for ignoring my instincts. These insights led me to appreciate the sanctity of the process. I realized that intuition is so special that it deserves the time and space to unfold naturally.

Chew on This . . .

Try this **Trust Your Taste Buds** exercise to help connect to your inner voice, enhance trust in your instincts, and create space for solutions to organically emerge.

- **CLEAR YOUR COUNTER:** Pause, close your eyes, take a deep breath, and come back to the present moment. Focus on the here and now and release external worries.

- **EXAMINE YOUR RECIPE:** Ask yourself a simple, open-ended question about your day, a decision, or a current problem or challenge to solve. For example:
  - What do I truly want from this experience or situation?
  - Why is this situation bothering me so much?
  - How does this choice or solution feel to me?
  - What is my instinct telling me about this next step?

- **LET IDEAS SIMMER:** Allow the answer to naturally arise. Avoid overthinking and racing for a rapid solution. Trust that your intuition often speaks subtly and needs time to arrive at the best solution.

- **TASTE-TEST YOUR CONCOCTION:** Transcribe or draw whatever comes to mind, whether it's a word, feeling, or symbol. It doesn't need to be fully formed since this is about honoring your instincts while allowing them to continue to simmer.

- **TO SERVE OR NOT TO SERVE:** Objectively decide whether you should act on your intuition immediately or allow it to continue simmering away. Either way, recognize the wisdom gained from this exercise and applaud your growth!

cherry on top
TRUSTING YOUR INNER COMPASS

Cultivating intuition is essential for any creative entrepreneur, unlocking deeper insights, guiding innovation, and helping navigate entrepreneurial challenges with finesse. A well-developed intuition allows you to anticipate trends, make better-informed decisions, and infuse your ventures with a distinctive vision that distinguishes you from others. While intuition is a skill that can be honed, it requires time and patience and cannot be oversimplified. There is no shortcut to intuition, which makes it all the more valuable and rewarding.

5

ASSESS AND ALTER YOUR RECIPE

Accessing and Allowing Feedback to Refine Your Concept

Here, you will determine if your recipe is truly ready to serve the world (meaning your solution effectively solves a real-world problem or your concept resonates with its target market). At this stage, you must consider your recipe or proposed solution to be merely a hypothesis that's awaiting actual consumer testing. Don't rely solely on your experience, reason, or logic; instead, present your idea to your target market to gather evidence of its reception and necessity. Be completely open to feedback and advice on how you can alter your concept to better fit the needs of your customer. This approach will enhance your chances of success and reveal hidden opportunities that might be overlooked by rigidly adhering to a predetermined business plan.

Verifying the deliciousness of your recipe (meaning the effectiveness of the solution to your problem to solve or target market appeal) includes two critical steps:

1. **ASSESS:** Honestly evaluate your recipe and decide if it is promising enough to invest further time and attention to refine it.

2. **ALTER:** Make changes to your recipe to better entice your target market.

STEP 1: ASSESS YOUR RECIPE

Not all creative ideas are effective solutions to the problem we're solving, and not all recipes are delicious enough to be printed on the permanent menu. Here is where you must rigorously assess whether your chef's-kiss recipe is worthy of being transformed into a dish that serves the world, which means that it is *both* innovative *and* something customers are eager to devour repeatedly. In this phase, you may come to realize that your current idea is unfortunately not the perfect recipe you thought it was when you conceived it. This is often the most emotionally trying part of the process, when you feel the most uncertain and insecure. It's also continually interrupted by additional periods of simmering that can produce more meaningful insights.

Maintaining that Start-from-Scratch mentality will allow many fresh insights to emerge, even as you put the finishing touches and garnishes on the initial insight. The recipe may become more nuanced, subtle, and intriguing, and perhaps even begin to manifest more elements of surprise and delight for the consumer. Above all, you must be brutally honest with yourself. Just because you personally find the recipe delicious doesn't mean it's delicious to others, and even if they find it delicious, that doesn't mean they'll crave it enough to choose it over other options and purchase it with their hard-earned money.

This is where all the knowledge you have internalized about your AOI, plus the opinions of your target market and/or knowledgeable mentors, takes on greater prominence. Is this recipe truly novel, or is it replicating an existing idea with major flaws and no appeal? What will your peers think of it? This is a period of intense assessment, self-criticism, and reflection, which takes overcoming one of the most challenging obstacles of the creative entrepreneurial process: fear of rejection and failure. You must be able to step back from *both* your recipe and your unhealthy ego to objectively assess its strengths and weaknesses and judge it for its taste, appearance, and originality.

If you decide that the recipe meets your criteria for a signature recipe and warrants further alteration, you will take it to the next step of the process. And if you determine that it's not worth a further investment of time and energy, you must reject it and choose to 1) renew your immersion in that same AOI and seek new problems to solve or new recipes to create, 2) pursue an entirely new AOI by gathering new ingredients and finding a brand-new problem to solve and new recipes to create, or 3) allow the existing ingredients more time to simmer and wait patiently for alternate (and more effective) solutions to emerge.

In order to assess your recipe, you'll need to ask the right assessment questions and create your key assessment criteria, such as a checklist.

Key Questions to Validate and Communicate Your Idea

If you believe that you have created an effective product or solution to your problem to solve, there are some essential questions to ask to ensure that you have fully embodied the problem and solution and can clearly articulate it to others. Your recipe details need to be communicated *just right* to become a product or service that sells like hotcakes. To communicate the importance of a new idea clearly and emphatically, you must be able to pull at people's heartstrings and articulately convey the genesis of your mission, its context, and where it fits in the world. If you can passionately illustrate its relationship to concepts people are familiar with, understand, and appreciate, it may convince them to embrace the idea. Possible questions include:

- What problem does your product/service tackle, and why does it get you out of bed every morning?

- How do you determine or know if the issue you're addressing is widespread?

- In what concrete ways does your product/service stand out with its unique features and benefits from existing offerings that address your problem to solve? How does it improve a customer's experience and differentiate itself in a crowded market? And why should customers invest their money in your product over your competitors' offerings?

- Can you simplify your value proposition enough for a child to grasp it? How will your product/service enhance individual people's lives, and what is your ultimate aspiration for it? What do you hope to achieve in the long term, and how does this align with your broader mission?

- How do you identify your target market experiencing the same problem and seeking your product/service? Who exactly are they? What are their needs, pain points, and preferences in brands and experiences?

- Who are your competitors?

- How will you position your product/service so your target market becomes aware of it? Where does it live in the world? What market? What category or area of life? Is it a niche or a mass product/service?

- Through what channels will your target market access and purchase it?

- Is your pricing accessible or premium? If it's a tangible product, is it manufactured in the United States or elsewhere? Is it sustainable, organic, both, or neither?

Product and Brand Assessment Checklist

In creating thousands of products for M&D, I needed a simple method to gauge if my concept was truly unique in comparison to what already existed in the market. Once my distinct vision for the product was clearly defined, I created the following checklist to determine if and how it stood apart from the competition. Although these principles largely apply to consumer products and packaging, they may also be used as a general framework to think about formulations, technologies, or services. My goal wasn't to fulfill every one of these criteria, but achieving *at least two of them* was necessary to move a product forward. And if I could somehow tick off all seven, I felt 100 percent confident that the product would be a success!

Your personal practice of appraising products and services may include the following considerations that became my timeworn recipe:

- **DESIGN:** Is your product/service differentiated enough in design over what currently exists in the market to cut through the clutter as original and appealing to the senses?

- **CUSTOMER EXPERIENCE:** Does your product/service offer an extraordinary consumer experience from start to finish that sets it apart from its competitors?

- **VALUE/ACCESSIBILITY:** Does your product/service offer pricing that allows it to get into as many hands as possible, provide significant value at every price point, and deliver multitudes of value-adding features and content?

- **QUALITY/SAFETY:** Is your product/service durably built and made to deliver safe, consistent, peak product performance throughout its life, from first use to last?

- **BRAND STORY:** Does your brand have a compelling, authentic, and emotional story communicating the why of your creation and how you personally combined your ingredients to create this original recipe?

- **SELECTION/BREADTH OF OFFERING:** Does your brand offer a wide enough selection to meet all a consumer's needs in a category, making them choose it over other competitors?

- **MERCHANDISING/MARKETING:** Does your brand have effective merchandising and compelling marketing content to draw target consumers and/or retailers into your net?

Answering these questions will help you assess the original recipe and determine if you need to change ingredient proportions, add additional ingredients from the pantry, or eliminate others in the next attempt to enhance it. If these criteria don't apply to your unique offering, create your own key assessment criteria based on the nuances of your product or service. Your ultimate goal is to determine whether your recipe is enticing and your brand is compelling enough to turn consumers into loyal repeat purchasers who eagerly share their love for your brand with others.

STEP 2: ALTER YOUR RECIPE—REFINING IDEAS INTO MASTERPIECES

Recipes and ideas must be altered to transform them into full-fledged dishes and offerings that others find appealing enough to order—and want to order again. After you've completed your assessment checklist, it's time to change anything that may need adjustment in order to meet your customers' needs. At the end of a successful alteration period, you should have a finished and winning recipe. These alterations may run the gamut from minor to major, and this stage may extend from either a few minutes to many months or years, depending on how much modification is needed.

First, this involves taking the very honest critique you obtained from the assessment process and determining which specific refinements you will make to your existing recipe. This stage can be extremely trying and takes a great deal of intense, hard work to fine-tune your recipe into its best possible form. You may feel that your recipe isn't measuring up to expectations and what you thought was a masterpiece now seems to be completely flawed. As you keep digging deeper, you may observe more imperfections that you were initially unaware of and realize that the recipe isn't delivering the kind of experience you had desired. You now must engage in painstaking, focused attention to the minute details to hone your recipe, which often involves conducting extensive taste-testing trials and gathering feedback to assess and reassess its quality. In the cases where your recipe is falling short, you may need to spend additional time talking with experienced chefs to gain more insight about what's considered exceptional in your category so you can then modify your product/service to better meet those standards.

The process of utilizing feedback is very straightforward and follows seven simple steps: being open to receiving feedback, asking for constructive feedback, mindfully finding your advisor/mentor, considering your timing for when to seek feedback, carefully evaluating that feedback, implementing the feedback that is most relevant, and showing appreciation for your mentors. We'll go into each of these steps throughout the rest of this chapter.

BENEFITS OF WELCOMING FEEDBACK

Until now, the product vision has been entirely your own, without any outside input. However, now is when you must welcome others into your kitchen to help you stir your pot. Your idea or concept will never be perfected until you're willing to invite *both* seasoned cooks and passionate foodies into your kitchen to taste-test your recipe. Only then can you accurately assess, then alter and refine your recipe to find its ideal resonance with your target market. Here, we see that "the proof is in the pudding," highlighting that only by trying the recipe can you determine if it's good or not.

Market feedback on your recipe is vital to ensure that it appeals to and delights your target market. When embraced and applied effectively, feedback offers several key benefits, including preventing costly mistakes and market failures by helping identify potential issues before launch, boosting innovation by sparking new ideas and approaches, fostering innovation and creativity, and ensuring that your product/service resonates with real people by aligning it with the target market's actual needs and preferences. Feedback also helps you uncover blind spots by offering fresh perspectives that can reveal flaws or opportunities that you might overlook, enhance quality by providing specific insights that help refine and improve your product/service, and build trust and credibility by showing your desire to engage with users and commit to excellence and responsiveness.

During this stage of inviting cooks into our kitchen, we must heed the adage "Too many cooks spoil the broth" and avoid involving so many people that it leads to confusion and poor results. If you have the courage to seek feedback, you will find that both experts in the field and target market consumers are enthusiastic about trying your recipe and providing detailed insights on how you can enhance it.

Being Open to Feedback (OTF)

Being open to honest feedback is essential for creating concepts that meet and exceed expectations and for making meaningful progress. Without the mindset and the willingness to seek, embrace, and utilize feedback—both from seasoned mentors and target market consumers—our efforts risk falling short of their full potential. However, despite its critical importance, most people are sensitive to criticism, which is natural given our inherent need for acceptance and validation. Being critiqued can challenge our self-esteem and self-worth, triggering feelings of inadequacy or fear of rejection.

If an entrepreneur struggles with feelings of inadequacy or is ashamed about their perceived lack of achievements, they may become especially defensive when criticized. They may try to lighten the blow to their ego by criticizing the person who critiqued them, vigorously defending themselves, or simply ignoring the person altogether. In these instances, the desire to protect their self-image outweighs the value of constructive criticism.

Furthermore, many entrepreneurs believe that they are the sole authorities on decisions regarding their product or service. This unhealthy ego bias can obscure our ability to seek valuable insights from experts or users in our field. Driven by confirmation bias and the tendency to favor our own opinions, regardless of their accuracy, we complicate our ability to objectively assess our competence. This often leads to an overreliance on intuition and results in overconfidence and decision-making based on preexisting beliefs. We tend to seek out information that confirms our views while unconsciously ignoring contradictory evidence. This bias protects our self-esteem and shields us from the fear of criticism. As a result, seeking feedback becomes daunting, as it might expose significant flaws in our cherished ideas. Consequently, we either avoid seeking feedback altogether or selectively seek validation for our ideas as they are, missing out on valuable perspectives from consumers and experienced mentors.

Even when entrepreneurs express a desire for feedback, they often fail to truly listen. Despite recognizing their limited expertise, they prioritize their own opinions over others' and struggle to understand the reasoning behind the feedback. Their rigid judgments prevent them from altering their approach, making them resistant to incorporating constructive criticism. Opening yourself up to receiving honest feedback—dispassionately and objectively—is vital. You may feel terrified of receiving critiques from mentors, as such feedback can feel like a personal rejection, challenging your vision and undermining your confidence in your product. The emotional investment and pride you have in your work make criticism especially daunting, as it exposes potential flaws and risks and validates your fears of failure. When you are deeply invested in your concept, it can be difficult to separate your emotions from the critique.

Moreover, the pressure to meet expectations coupled with uncertainty about how to address the feedback can heighten anxiety, making the prospect of receiving critiques both stressful and overwhelming. While it's crucial for entrepreneurs to become comfortable with actively seeking, accepting, and embracing constructive criticism, doing so remains one of the most challenging aspects of entrepreneurship. That being said, becoming OTF is a skill that can be developed and honed through deliberate practice!

Story Nugget

An author sent a list of possible book titles to a group of fellow writers, asking which one they liked best. It was fascinating to see that the request was only to select a favorite among the provided list, not to offer broader comments or suggest alternative titles. Instead, we were simply asked to choose our preferred title from the short list provided. As a totally objective mentor, I felt strongly that none of the titles felt perfectly suited to the narrative or appropriately compelling. I shared my thoughts and excitedly suggested a new "perfect title," certain that it best encapsulated the book's message. However, in the end, the author chose a title from that original list. I found myself surprisingly annoyed that I had spent valuable time brainstorming alternative options, especially since it became clear that they never intended to utilize anyone else's input.

This situation highlighted that their request for feedback might have been aimed not at finding the best options or improving upon them but rather at validating an already-favored choice. It appeared that there was a strong confirmation bias going in, with the author already knowing which title they were leaning toward. Ultimately, making the decision was the author's prerogative, but the feedback request seemed more about personal affirmation than seeking genuine input to refine the product.

A Taste of Practice

Your personal practice to become OTF and remain nonjudgmental while taking in face-value critiques of your recipe may include:

- **APPRECIATING THAT ALL IDEAS ARE DERIVATIVE** and recognizing that they are already recombining existing ingredients. This means you are already using other people's ideas! Granted, you may not personally know those people, but they have helped you conceive your product. Mark Twain eloquently expressed, "There is no such thing as a new idea. It is impossible. We simply take a lot of old ideas and put them into a sort of mental kaleidoscope. We give them a turn and they make new and curious combinations. We keep on turning and making new combinations indefinitely; but they are the same old pieces of colored glass that have been in use through all the ages."[1] Isaac Newton observed that we all "stand on the shoulders of giants," expanding on the knowledge, discoveries, and achievements of those who came before us.[2] Therefore, you should welcome others' input, knowing that their work offers additional fresh ingredients. Gathering as many different ingredients as possible from diverse perspectives creates the best-tasting, most innovative recipes.

- **CULTIVATING A GROWTH MINDSET** and embracing the belief that feedback is a tool for improvement rather than a personal attack. View critiques as opportunities to improve rather than as reflections of your worth. Ask yourself, "*How* is this feedback able to *help* me," rather than "*Why* is this feedback trying to *harm* me?"

- **SEPARATING YOURSELF FROM YOUR CREATION** and recognizing that feedback is about the product or idea, not you personally. This self-distancing helps you take critiques less personally and more constructively. Using the simmering process for feedback can further support self-distancing. Think of critical feedback as another key ingredient in your recipe—mix it with your other ingredients and let them all settle into the subconscious and recombine. Soon, they will organically give rise to revelations and new ideas!

- **PRACTICING ACTIVE LISTENING AND RESPONDING WITH CURIOSITY,** focusing on truly understanding the feedback given rather than immediately defending your work. This includes asking clarifying questions and hearing specific examples with concrete suggestions to better understand where the critique is coming from and how to improve, ensuring that you grasp the full context of the feedback and can assess it dispassionately.

- **ACKNOWLEDGING AND ACCEPTING EMOTIONS,** knowing that it's natural to feel defensive or emotional about feedback. Acknowledge these feelings without letting them cloud your judgment, and take time to let them flow through you and out. Only then will you be able to process the feedback responsively, not reactively.

- **SEEKING FEEDBACK REGULARLY,** understanding that the more you expose yourself to feedback, the more comfortable you'll become with it. Regularly asking for and receiving feedback helps normalize the process and highlight its importance in perfecting your product.

- **REFLECTING, ANALYZING,** and taking time to assess the feedback's validity and relevance to your mission and goals. Consider how it aligns with your vision and how it can enhance your product/service.

- **BUILDING A SUPPORTIVE ENVIRONMENT** by surrounding yourself with people who provide honest, constructive feedback and are supportive in helping you grow. This helps you to trust the process and make the entire feedback experience more positive.

A Full Serving of Practice

Being a perfectionist made it extremely challenging for me to accept feedback early in life. However, as a toy designer, I realized how essential feedback was to my process since I was creating products for children, not for myself. Ultimately, my most transformative feedback came from my own children evaluating these playthings. Early on, they were fearful of being completely honest and telling me the truth. It was clear that they didn't want to say something that came across as "mean," nor did they want to hurt my feelings. Yet the more I came to value the power of honest feedback and the better I communicated that desire to them, the more they started delivering the truth. And although their assessments were, at times, agonizing to hear, they were likewise instrumental in helping me refine my ideas to create a better overall customer experience and the foundation for a trusted brand.

One of their comments was on an interactive game that came with four stuffed frogs. I thought the frogs were absolutely adorable when I viewed their cute, friendly faces from the side. But when my daughter examined one of the frogs head-on, as if greeting a person, she immediately threw it on the floor with a gasp and said, "I don't like that frog; he looks angry."

I had been ready to give this product my final approval before production, and her comment, seemingly so minor, frustrated me. I replied dismissively, "What do you mean? He's a perfectly happy frog!" But then, I examined the frog head-on myself and was shocked to see that it indeed looked very angry—like scary angry! I instructed our team to delay production to make the frog's mouth look more amiable. After all, we wanted these creatures to become comforting best friends for children!

Chew on This . . .

Try this **Savor the Feedback Formula** to reinforce the habit of welcoming feedback, constructively processing it, and using it as a tool for continual growth.

- **A FRESH FLAVOR A DAY:** Ask one person every day for honest feedback on something you've made, created, done, or brainstormed, no matter how lofty.

- **EXTRACT THE ESSENCE:** Mine the feedback for what it taught you or what you learned rather than how you felt about it. Transcribe that insight in a journal or notes app.

- **REFINE TO ENHANCE:** Consider if and how the feedback can help improve your recipe. If it doesn't seem relevant, think about why and how you can improve the process going forward.

- **SEASON WITH GRATITUDE:** Recognize one thing you're grateful for from receiving the feedback. It could be appreciation for the honesty, gaining a new perspective, or having the opportunity to hear the feedback dispassionately and accept it wholeheartedly.

Asking for Constructive Feedback

Learning how to effectively ask for constructive feedback is a skill that requires practice and intentionality. Most people are fearful of hurting our feelings, so to counter this, I coined the rhyme "*Beg for the neg*(ative)" as a reminder that critical feedback is often the most valuable feedback. If we ask questions that elicit overly general or excessively positive responses, we miss out on the genuine opinions and beliefs that could help refine our concept. To gather valuable, concrete insights, it's crucial to frame your questions in a way that elicits detailed and actionable responses.

Here are tips on how to ask for honest and useful feedback:

BE SPECIFIC: General questions like "What do you think of my idea?" are often too broad and can lead to vague or unhelpful answers. Instead, ask targeted questions that address specific aspects of your product or concept. For example, a question like "What are three things you would change about this concept?" directs the respondent to focus on specific elements, providing more actionable feedback.

SEEK PRACTICAL INSIGHTS: Ask questions that reveal practical, quantitative information about the product's/service's market potential. For instance, a question like "How much would you ideally pay for this item?" helps you gauge pricing expectations and perceived value, which is critical for effective positioning. This approach is more effective than simply stating a retail price and asking, "Would you purchase this for X?"

UNDERSTAND NEEDS AND PREFERENCES: To improve your product, consider what additional features or changes would enhance its value. Questions like "What specific elements need to be added or deleted to improve this product?" prompt respondents to think about improvements from their perspective, which can be crucial for refinement.

GAUGE PURCHASING INTENT: Determine how well your product aligns with the needs of your target market by asking if they would consider purchasing it. For example, a question like "Would you purchase this product for yourself, as a gift for others, or both? Why or why not?" helps you understand its appeal and potential market fit.

ENCOURAGE DETAILED FEEDBACK: Encourage respondents to provide detailed explanations rather than just yes-or-no answers. This can be done by avoiding yes-or-no questions and requesting, even imploring, that they elaborate on their suggestions or describe specific scenarios in which the product might excel or fall short.

By asking focused, direct questions and encouraging detailed, practical feedback, you can gain valuable insights that directly inform your product development and marketing strategy.

Story Nugget

Feedback was essential to M&D's process of creating exceptional playthings. So essential that we created a detailed retailer feedback survey for salespeople to complete during our largest trade show, the New York Toy Fair, where we introduced our newest products. After each selling day, our salespeople transcribed the un-sugarcoated customer feedback they had obtained from retailers on our new products. Each item received a letter grade and ranking, along with in-depth comments.

I read every word of these daily assessments, using them to ultimately categorize our products into three groups: clear winners for immediate mass production, well-received items with potential that needed modifications before mass production, and products that didn't have market fit and would not progress further. We delivered these results in a full product development (PD) team wrap-up after the trade show. These meetings became the cornerstone of our PD calendar for the year. As in any competition, the teams working on these ideas anxiously awaited to hear if their idea made it to the next round. These surveys became invaluable in guiding my PD process, acting in concert with my intuition to help determine the direction to take and the changes and modifications needed to refine those products.

MINDFULLY FINDING YOUR ADVISOR/MENTOR

Finding an appropriate advisor/mentor to become a sounding board can be incredibly difficult. You must be especially mindful as to which cooks you invite into the kitchen, knowing ones with different tastes and experiences could easily "stir the pot" and taint your recipe and/or confuse your authentic vision.

Your advisor will ideally have a consistent, proven track record in your AOI or specific niche. It is essential to deeply understand the individuals from whom you seek advice, for experience has taught me that *it is far better to have no advisor at all than a poor one*. This means you must be patient, reach out to and meet with lots of different people, and "cherry-pick" the very best. Before considering their counsel, ask them to share their relevant experience and the specific results demonstrating their success. The most valuable advisors are those who have achieved consistent success in your field.

Also, remember to take all feedback "with a grain of salt." This implies that although the suggestion may have some validity, it should be viewed or interpreted with skepticism or caution, recognizing that it may not be completely accurate or reliable. Essentially, it suggests that you should never take input at face value and be prepared for the possibility that it might be exaggerated, incomplete, or even deceptive. This is because, although some advisors/mentors are gems, most generally fall into one of two opposing camps: advisors/mentors who do not provide *useful* feedback and advisors/mentors who do not provide *honest* feedback.

Advisors/Mentors Not Providing *Useful* Feedback

Many mentors don't offer useful advice, largely because they don't take the time to really understand your unique AOI or recipe. Therefore, they are prone to misunderstanding the problems you are facing rather than gaining a true understanding of the situation. Without a good sense of your business, mentors will give feedback solely from their experiences and frame of reference. Excessive reliance on existing solutions by advisors can lead to oversight of crucial details and the inability to customize recommendations that suit your unique requirements. It is well-known that leaning heavily on conventional options generally stifles innovation and creativity. Instead of challenging existing ideas, helping brainstorm alternative solutions, or encouraging you to push boundaries, some mentors might offer quick fixes that don't match your venture's long-term goals or vision.

In essence, this means that some advisors won't change their way of thinking based on the unique tenets and circumstances of your product or venture. Rather, they will quickly jump to premature conclusions because they *think* they see similarities with the challenges they've faced. Or they'll give inadequate answers based on a limited amount of information or partial account, which biases their responses. These incomplete accounts lead to inaccurate assessments and, thus, flawed advice.

Many of our M&D mentors believed us to be a premium brand, when in actuality we were a premium-quality mass-market brand. If a mentor has an incorrect perception and doesn't take the time to learn about your business, they will give you recommendations based exclusively on their prior experience. If their experience is relevant to your business, it may prove worthwhile, but if not, it will be entirely useless. Someone who has been a surgeon may have valuable insights, but they probably won't be applicable to someone creating and manufacturing food products. Therefore, it is critical to assess whether an advisor "is your cup of tea" or not, only seeking feedback from those whose experience and ethos best align with your core tenets. This means you may need to gently say "no thanks" after a meeting or two with some well-meaning advisors. I have had to say those two words many times!

Doug and I had the privilege of working with an exceptional group of business leaders as M&D grew. Their vast experience and impressive track records marked them as elite masters in their fields, and we were in awe of their achievements. We eagerly anticipated leveraging their wisdom to address our most pressing business challenges. We prepared a list of critical questions for our first advisory meeting, seeking their astute counsel on so many thorny topics. However, we were shocked by their reaction upon posing our first question: whether we needed to develop distinct product lines for different markets. They looked at us blankly, replying, "Wow, that's an excellent and very difficult question! What's your gut on that?"

Doug and I exchanged brief, panicked glances that silently questioned, "What is happening here? Why aren't they providing us with the answers we need?" It quickly became apparent that they were just as uncertain as we were—perhaps even less equipped to offer definitive solutions given their experience in vastly different industries. In that moment, it hit us: we were largely on our own, left to rely on our own experience and intuition to navigate these difficult questions.

In truth, these leaders had led their companies decades before we did, and those companies were in entirely different industries than ours with completely distinct target markets. Moreover, their demanding personal and professional commitments left them with little time to immerse themselves in the toy industry to truly understand our unique perspective and priorities. As a result, they were not well-positioned to provide the guidance we sought. Nonetheless, they frequently offered strong opinions and pressed us to focus on what mattered *to them* rather than what aligned with our vision. They consistently offered recommendations, like raising our accessible prices, adopting a licensing strategy, or avoiding selling on Amazon.com because it would denigrate our brand. These suggestions often seemed out of sync with our ethos, and it turned out that many of them were. Amazon, for one, became our biggest and most important customer, elevating our exposure and brand cachet through its reviews and reach!

I frequently find myself needing to counteract advice given to my entrepreneurs by so-called experts who lack relevant experience—such as well-meaning, conservative parents who offer general cautionary advice that lacks specifics and warns against taking any of the risks associated with entrepreneurship or individuals who have achieved success but are from entirely different industries and have no knowledge of or expertise in a different AOI.

It's essential to thoroughly vet your advisors to ensure their backgrounds and experiences align with the *specific* challenges you're currently facing. Be cautious of taking advice from those who either don't have direct experience in your field or may have had direct experience decades ago when the market was entirely different. Additionally, seek feedback from individuals who match your target market profile. For instance, if your product is designed for preschool children, focus on insights from parents of young children rather than those who have older kids or no children at all. The more closely you align your advisors with your existing issues and customer base, the more valuable and applicable their feedback will be.

Advisors/Mentors Not Providing *Honest* Feedback

On the other side of the equation are advisors/mentors who are terrified to dole out honest feedback. It's the whole white-lie phenomenon—a small lie told to be polite or avoid hurting someone's feelings. There are many reasons why some advisors don't give honest feedback. They may not want to seem like they're a know-it-all, or they could be unsure how to give constructive criticism. Perhaps they don't want to risk upsetting you, damaging the relationship, and hurting feelings. Maybe they don't want to risk that you will reject both the feedback and them or prove them wrong.

In other instances, mentors may not trust the quality of their feedback, or perhaps they don't think it's truly valuable and will help you. They don't want to jeopardize their expert status and risk looking incompetent. Yet without asking probing questions and having full knowledge of your business, they cannot give genuine feedback. Some mentors are self-absorbed and offer self-centered guidance based on how they would respond if they were in your shoes. They don't know or think about how you feel and end up acting without any sense of empathy.

Often, these kinds of mentors don't know how or where to best support you with a concrete action plan. Thus, they offer too many ideas, options, plans, and perspectives without any guidance on how to narrow down the list. This can lead to paralysis. Lastly, there are those with fragile egos who take offense and sulk or disappear when you don't heed their advice. They don't know their place and lack self-awareness. Therefore, they give unsolicited advice and overstep their boundaries. They also offer recommendations that are much too general, use big words that you don't remotely understand, and tend to interrupt just for ego's sake when they have no qualifications to do so. This makes you unable to trust them and drives you to question their credibility. It is critical that you steer clear of these types of advisors/mentors and seek out those who inspire confidence and help you grow with genuine, thoughtful guidance. The right mentors will respect your journey and empower you to reach your full potential.

CONSIDERING YOUR TIMING FOR WHEN TO SEEK FEEDBACK

It's important to seek feedback on your recipe at precisely the right time: neither too early nor too late. If you invite others to stir your pot too early in the process before your soup stock/vision is clarified, you risk becoming confused and utilizing input that could taint or overshadow your unique perspective. Ensure that your concept is fully developed and aligns with your distinct vision before seeking external opinions.

On the other hand, waiting too long to gather feedback may delay product launches and disappoint customers. This creates a reluctance to utilize the advice and make the necessary and meaningful changes. Aim to strike a balance where feedback can refine and enhance your vision without compromising its originality or timeliness.

For example, we received production samples for our new Lifelines flameless candle aroma diffuser too close to the promised delivery date to retailers to make significant adjustments. However, we had concurrently received insightful yet disappointing feedback from an employee tester, highlighting significant functional issues that negatively impacted the user experience. My first thought upon reading her write-up was *There's no way we have time to fix all these problems and still hit our ship schedule!* For a split second, I wondered, *Should we let the product go out as is to hit our ship date and fix these issues later?*

However, I knew I could never forgive myself if I knowingly put out a flawed product. Therefore, I took a deep breath and forwarded the verbatim critique to our engineering team with the heading "Need to fix all these issues *before* releasing to mass production." And yes, making these changes delayed our launch and led to lost orders and difficult conversations with retailers, but I firmly believe we had no other option.

The issue of delays frequently arises because the PD process, especially for complex items, tends to run late, with first prototypes arriving just before mass production. By then, the product is often already promised to retailers, leaving no time for changes without delaying the shipment. Despite these circumstances, my conscience prevents me from releasing a faulty product when improvements are possible. As a result, we have had no choice but to introduce many products later than initially promised, driven by our commitment to perfecting them. We understood that disappointing our customers with delays was unacceptable while also recognizing that gathering and implementing feedback was crucial.

We ultimately revamped our M&D PD process to integrate "collecting feedback" into our schedule and ensured that we received samples early enough to incorporate insights and improvements before the product went into mass production. We are now making the very same process improvement changes at Lifelines, given that we have already missed hitting retailer ship dates on multiple launches and incurred financial penalties (called chargebacks)!

In addition to neglecting the simmering process, entrepreneurs tend to avoid asking for and/or utilizing market data and feedback and investing sufficient effort into refining and perfecting their concepts. They may feel like they've already put so much effort into an idea that they're eager to push forward without revisiting or revising it. The thought of stopping to make changes, which requires additional time and resources, can be overwhelming. This is due to that rush mentality and wanting to race ahead with a finished product, an obstacle that can overshadow the pursuit of excellence and hamper one's ability to produce extraordinary work. That being said, all that really matters in an entrepreneurial venture is the caliber of the product/service and nothing more. Everything else is secondary, and there will be no phase two or future for your venture without creating an extraordinary product today.

At M&D, our graphic designers frequently presented me with packaging or artwork that I found unsatisfactory. When asked to revise it—despite being on company time—they'd express annoyance, often saying, "But I'm already finished with this mentally and emotionally and ready to move on!" I found this response exasperating since the result wasn't remotely up to our standards. I, therefore, strongly pushed the designers to refine their work and graciously make the necessary improvements. And in thirty-five years of comparing before-and-after results, there was not a single instance where the revisions didn't lead to a significantly enhanced product.

CAREFULLY EVALUATING THE FEEDBACK

Carefully evaluate all your market feedback, using your intuition and distinct perspective to stay true to your original concept. During this process, it's essential to retain only the most valuable and relevant insights and discard the rest to preserve your idea's integrity. However, sifting through feedback is another difficult aspect of creating an extraordinary product/service. To manage extensive feedback effectively while maintaining your core vision, follow these steps:

- **ORGANIZE AND CATEGORIZE:** Sort feedback into categories based on common themes or issues to help identify patterns and prioritize the most relevant comments.

- **FILTER FOR THE MOST IMPACTFUL:** Zero in on feedback that aligns with your core vision and goals, and dismiss suggestions that deviate from your main concept or are not feasible within your current resource constraints.

- **EVALUATE CREDIBILITY:** Assess the credibility of the feedback sources, prioritizing insights from those with current, relevant experience or who accurately fit your target market profile.

- **BALANCE FEEDBACK WITH VISION:** Evaluate how each piece of feedback aligns with your original concept using your distinct perspective, ensuring that changes suggested by feedback improve, rather than fundamentally alter, your core idea.

- **PRIORITIZE KEY INSIGHTS:** Focus on insights that will meaningfully improve your product's success, identifying and prioritizing feedback that offers readily actionable, high-impact improvements.

- **TRUST YOUR INTUITION:** Use your intuition to gauge which pieces of feedback most resonate with your vision and goals. Your intuition and clear understanding of your concept will help you discern which suggestions to incorporate.

- **REVIEW AND REFLECT:** Regularly review the feedback you utilized and reflect on if and how it influenced your product. Then adjust your approach based on what's working and what's not, all the while staying true to your core concept.

IMPLEMENTING THE MOST RELEVANT FEEDBACK

Once you've cherry-picked your most salient feedback morsels, implement those relevant improvements on a small scale to witness how they affect your recipe. An iterative approach allows you to test changes and verify their alignment with your vision before fully implementing them. Then, you may be ready to assess if your concept is "good enough" to put out into the world. Many entrepreneurs fear either going all in on their single idea or launching it into the world—often paralyzed by a fear of not achieving perfection. This fear often keeps them stuck as dreamers and tinkerers without taking action.

When releasing new toys for production, I always followed what I called the 80 percent rule. I would give new toys the go-ahead once they met all my criteria and I could think of no further improvements. I knew they were still imperfect, but they were as refined as possible without getting actual market feedback. I considered them about 80 percent complete—an acceptance rate that was challenging for a perfectionist but necessary to get them out into the world, with further refinements coming from real user data once the product was in the market. Striving for 100 percent perfection would mean never releasing them at all, and I preferred launching a product that was less than perfect to never letting it see the light of day.

At M&D and now at Lifelines, we continually improve our products after release based on field data. As a recovering perfectionist, I now use the verb "perfecting" to describe the ongoing, active process of continually improving my products, knowing that perfection is always out of reach. This iterative perfecting process moves us closer to 100 percent over time. This is why many iconic consumer products, like paper towels and ketchup, boast labels highlighting "new and improved." Continuous enhancement is key. Every product I develop remains in a state of ongoing improvement, never reaching perfection but always evolving closer to it with new knowledge, perspectives, wisdom, and consumer usage feedback.

SHOWING APPRECIATION FOR YOUR ADVISORS/MENTORS

If you are fortunate enough to find a seasoned cook who is willing to test your concept and give you honest feedback, hold on to them with all your might. Not many people are willing to offer their hearts and minds to someone else voluntarily, as it is a big commitment of time and energy. When you find that special someone, it is essential to engage in the following steps to show them how much you appreciate the relationship and your commitment to helping it grow.

- Communicate exactly why you selected *them specifically* to be your mentor. How does their life experience uniquely relate to what you are doing?

- Make them feel as if they are specially qualified to help with your unique venture.

- Create an agenda for every meeting and come prepared with a robust list of questions.

- Respect your mentor's allotted time and always be punctual for your meetings. Acknowledge that the session will be ending a few minutes prior to the end time.

- Send your mentor personal, handwritten thank-you notes after every meeting, highlighting aspects of the conversation that were especially meaningful. Thank them profusely for giving you their precious time, which is truly a gift.

- Convey exactly which bits of your mentor's advice changed your thinking and your go-forward strategy. Share concrete examples of how you have utilized their guidance, and discuss your milestones and long-term goals with them.

The more you can personalize the mentor/mentee relationship and show your mentors how important they are to you, the more they will want to give of themselves to support you. I know this because I have lived it for fifteen years. If I feel uniquely irreplaceable and truly needed, I am willing to go to the moon for my entrepreneurs. But if they miss meetings without an excuse, don't come to meetings prepared, never take the advice to heart, or rarely utilize any of the discussion points to make forward strides in their business, we both soon lose interest in continuing the relationship.

Over half of those I've mentored fall into the category of being short-term, casual relationships, where we converse once or twice with little follow-up. About a third go through the motions of building a meaningful mentor/mentee relationship, but they don't seem genuinely engaged, don't ask salient questions, and don't meaningfully move their ventures forward. Therefore, the relationship soon fizzles out. Then, there are the handful of entrepreneurs whom I have continuously mentored for over a decade. These individuals have all engaged in roughly the same behavior of steadfastly building both their ventures and our relationship. Maybe 5 to 10 percent fall into this quintessential mentor/mentee relationship status, and I treasure these connections like precious jewels!

DISTRACTIONS FROM PERFECTING YOUR RECIPE

As we come to the end of our discussion on seeking and utilizing feedback to alter your recipe, it's important to understand the potential obstacles. Why do entrepreneurs tend to become distracted from accessing and utilizing feedback to create extraordinary recipes?

Flavor-of-the-Month Syndrome

As humans, our eyes are naturally drawn to the thrill of what delicious new flavor is next to debut: a chance to align with someone with more followers than we have, a fresh trend, or an entirely novel idea. We become enamored with and distracted by all the new, enticing, delicious flavors displayed right before our eyes that seem to promise quick and easy wins and immediate revenues rather than focusing single-mindedly on creating a product that sells like hotcakes. We behave like a child in a candy shop, scampering from bin to bin with erratic movements and abruptly changing direction in search of the next tempting treat.

Entrepreneurs also adopt this behavior when they don't know exactly what to do to advance their product or find it too challenging or terrifying to do the grueling work of refinement. They procrastinate and allow themselves to become distracted by all the easier, more fun, appealing areas that only become important *once* their incredible idea has been brought to life. They focus on everything *but* the product itself.

My entrepreneurs continually chase all the alluring, extrinsic rewards like gaining potential partnerships, creating cool logos or taglines, building their social media platforms and internal teams, securing the product/service's manufacturer or developer, or brainstorming adjacent ideas that would only make sense once their initial idea takes off. These are all necessary aspects of a successful business, but only *after* creating an exceptional recipe! I coined a phrase in our M&D Entrepreneurs program whenever a student came to us gushing about initiatives irrelevant to creating an extraordinary product and customer experience. I simply wagged my finger and admonished them, "Just focus on the product, dammit!"

Becoming enamored with how many new flavors we can devour actually prevents us from perfecting our original idea and honing the secret sauce that truly separates us from the crowd. Ask yourself, have you made your current product as good as you possibly can before serving it to the world and accessing their feedback? Imagine that this is the first or only product someone purchases from your company. Does it convey the essence of your brand and captivate consumers in the exact way you imagined?

Story Nugget

Early on, our team at Lifelines was eager to explore initiatives like collaborating with celebrities to feature their fragrances in our products and creating exclusive items for retailers. These opportunities are undeniably alluring and can seem straightforward to execute, but they often prove to be far more complex than they initially appear.

For instance, we are currently developing an exclusive product for a well-known retailer. While the project seemed simple at first, the retailer requested a unique type of packaging that proved difficult to source and later decided on a graphic style that deviated significantly from our established branding. Meeting these demands required an unexpected level of effort and resources. Considering the relatively small size of the opening order, this project nearly stretched us to our limit, especially given the ongoing demands of managing and growing our own product lines.

Over the years, I've learned that for start-ups, it's usually wiser to focus on building your own brand rather than dedicating limited resources to promote others' brands, unless there's a clear co-branding strategy in place. Without that strategy, there's a risk of diverting resources away from establishing your brand, often without securing the significant volume orders needed to justify the effort. If your brand has not yet achieved critical mass, avoid becoming someone else's product development department at the expense of your growth. Once your brand is thriving, these collaborative opportunities will naturally become easier to pursue and will be much more beneficial to your business.

That said, many entrepreneurs today operate under the belief that success hinges on forging partnerships and acquiring influencers early on. However, these partnerships should ideally result from your brand reaching a certain scale, not be an initial goal. As your brand grows, influencer partnerships will readily become more accessible, giving you a broader range of opportunities. This approach reflects my experience at M&D, where investing in quality products, customer experiences, and humble communication about our authentic mission ultimately created a groundswell of influencers and partners coming to us.

Chasing Quantity over Quality and Trying to Expand Too Quickly

Even when many entrepreneurs have a good idea, they are often looking to expand before they maximize all their opportunities with the product they have or fully refine the existing recipe. They get halfway down the path but don't wholly create a winning formula that is tested and honed until it becomes a flawless, repeatable model. There are numerous ways to maximize your idea before trying to grow beyond it and create completely new products.

Much of this need for increased quantity comes from ego-seeking validation and bragging rights regarding how many products, locations, partnerships, retail partners, or followers you have. But quantity doesn't necessarily equate to success since it's usually much more profitable to squeeze the most juice out of what you've already harvested than to incur the costs of more locations, more tooling, and more inventory.

This quality-over-quantity mindset also extends to needing to scale mindfully and strike a balance between growing and building out the necessary infrastructure to support that growth. Taking on *more* business than you are capable of handling well is another potential pitfall that will result in both a quality drain and a working capital drain. This puts many successful businesses out of business! And it's based not on a lack of sales but rather on too many sales and an inability to support them. This may overwhelm a small business and leave it unable to deliver and effectively serve its customers.

At M&D, I followed the 80 percent rule for expansion as well, avoiding entering new categories or territories until we had captured about 80 percent market share in our current one. We focused solely on designing puzzles for over a decade and didn't expand internationally until after two decades, when we maximized opportunities in the US market. While many manufacturers boast about their global reach, achieving profitability and critical mass abroad is resource-draining and challenging because each country operates differently. Rather than expanding for the sake of expansion, we ensured that we were dominant in one market before moving forward into the next. I also resisted premature expansion to avoid inviting competitors to replicate our ideas in untapped markets, effectively protecting both our territories and our innovation. Seeding a market with new ideas before establishing yourself as a strong leader is basically handing competitors your ideas to take and replicate!

Likewise, many M&D retailers sought growth by opening more stores, overlooking the fact that the personal connection they brought to their first store was the key differentiator. Expanding meant doubling inventory, rent, and labor—challenges they failed to anticipate. In my three decades of working with these retailers (and co-writing a training guide for independent toy store operators), I found that it was *always* more effective to offer additional services in an existing location or expand its size before opening additional locations. Owners typically lacked the same diligence in research, strategy, and planning for subsequent locations that they applied to their first.

The most successful retailers continually innovated within their existing space. For example, the franchise Learning Express expanded to serve different ages by adding gift sections for tweens and teens. Other retailers hosted birthday parties in their stores and extended hours for fundraising events. Some leveraged their existing inventory for e-commerce, offering delivery, gift-wrapping, and personalized shopping experiences. These efforts often required investing in point-of-sale and racking systems to support this omnichannel approach, yet they enabled retailers to maximize their current resources and grow sustainably.

Being Motivated by Extrinsic Rewards and Ease of Execution

Seeking extrinsic rewards leads some entrepreneurs to pursue ego-inflating prizes like speaking on panels, applying for awards and grants, hiring and managing bigger teams to gain more influence, securing prestigious partnerships, leasing beautiful workspaces, attending conferences to gain respect, and acting in ways to receive praise and recognition. Creative solutions to problems occur much more frequently when individuals engage in an activity for the sheer pleasure of doing so and it becomes autotelic rather than when they do so for potential external rewards. Extrinsic rewards should never lead the way in a heart-centric, mission-based venture and are counter to uncovering the heart of entrepreneurship. They are no doubt part of the equation, but you should always focus on doing what feels intuitively right for you, your product/service, and your customer. Heart decisions will always serve your mission more authentically than unhealthy ego decisions.

Entrepreneurs and their teams often gravitate toward the easiest and least challenging path, focusing on short-term gains or quick fixes. Recently, a Lifelines team member suggested simplifying our patented diffuser pen cartridge from four different scents to just one single scent that filled all four cartridges. This would have dramatically reduced costs and streamlined production; however, it also would have eliminated our key feature and patentable edge, making it quite ordinary and easier for competitors to replicate. Despite its manufacturing challenges, I knew it was essential to maintain the original design and protect our innovative spirit. While their suggestion highlighted efficiency, building something unique often requires navigating complexity and making decisions that prioritize long-term value over immediate convenience.

Becoming Distracted by Self-Absorption, Self-Focus, and Drama

Often, the human mind becomes so oversaturated with personal problems or others' drama that those problems displace our creative problems and prevent us from conceiving valuable insights and innovative solutions. Attachment to personal and external problems serves to keep us stuck in the past or the future. However, insights only arise in the present moment when the mind has enough air and space to allow ideas to combine and recombine and lead to epiphanies. Our problems clog our minds and suffocate our entrepreneurial hearts, preventing any fresh air from entering and recirculating. In these instances, there's no room or time left to simply let your mind simmer all those life-experience ingredients. There's no energy or openness to ideate, innovate, question, and allow the joy of life's extraordinary wonders to simply manifest each day.

In each class of M&D Entrepreneurs, there are generally one or two individuals who have a tremendous amount of drama occurring in their lives. This leaves them unable to effectively focus on their venture. When the mind is locked in self and personalizing everything that happens, it is apt to become consumed and obsessed with unsolvable problems and take on a victim mentality. All that happens becomes personal and something that's occurring *to* them rather than *for* them. They are unable to escape that loop, missing deadlines and neglecting to forward their progress during the program.

Likewise, there are others who face similar challenges and conflict in their lives but still manage to compartmentalize and maintain focus on their ventures. They appear to have a high level of resilience, discipline, and often a strong support system. These students might use various strategies like setting clear boundaries, practicing mindfulness, or using innate fortitude to prevent their personal difficulties from hindering their venture objectives. Not to mention, their dedication to pushing forward despite obstacles provides a powerful example of perseverance and effective focus for other entrepreneurs in the program.

A Taste of Practice

Your personal practice to manage personal and team-related issues without letting them derail your focus or productivity may include:

- **TIME-BLOCKING TO SET BOUNDARIES** by designating specific times during each day to deal with personal issues. I like to do this either first thing in the morning or at the end of the day. Once you identify a time that works best for you, consciously put aside all distractions and focus entirely on your venture. This will help prevent problems from spilling into your work hours and enable you to give your best during the bulk of the day and move your business forward.

- **ADOPTING THE FIVE-MINUTE RULE** to speed up your decision-making time whenever you experience a problem. Allocating a set time to ruminate on a problem can prevent you from spiraling into overthinking. After those five minutes, decide whether you need to immediately address the issue or wait until your designated time block. This rule helps prevent small problems from becoming large distractions.

- **CREATING TRANSITION ROUTINES** to help you return to your work and disconnect from the drama after you have dealt with a personal issue. You may take a walk, draw, listen to music, or deep breathe. These brief breaks will help clear and reset your mind and body, creating space for you to focus on your entrepreneurial responsibilities.

- **JOURNALING YOUR PROBLEMS** by listing them and explaining their nature under the heading "Problems to Solve." This allows you to externalize the problem, staying aware of it but putting it aside until later. Knowing that it's captured can help release the anxiety of holding on to it while you concentrate on your work.

- **FINDING AN ACCOUNTABILITY BUDDY** you can confide in about your challenge to compartmentalize, then having them regularly check on you to make certain that you're not letting it consume you.

- **CREATING MOTIVATING, UPLIFTING QUOTES** to remind you to stay the course throughout the week. When outside distractions arise, read over these notes to help you refocus on what's important and block out distractions. I constantly repeat to myself, "I can only create in the present moment." This reminds me to stay focused and present in the here and now and keep channeling.

A Full Serving of Practice

Learning how to time-block completely changed my life. Before then, I would spend the majority of my days ruminating over personal matters. And with six children, my life strongly followed the motto "You're only as happy as your least happy child." There was always someone to be worrying about or something not going as planned. I started time-blocking by choosing my ideal time of day to address personal issues. Usually it was the first thirty to sixty minutes of the day for existing issues, and if new problems arose during the day, I would dedicate the last thirty to sixty minutes of the day to handling them.

To create consistency, I would add the time block to my daily calendar, which reinforced the habit and helped make it stick. At the beginning, I would even set alarms to make certain that I transitioned into and out of this time block. I also designated a few special spaces I could retreat to and ensure that I eliminated distractions. In the mornings, that space was outdoors in nature. I nearly always used walking to ponder personal problems since nature swiftly grounded me and helped me think more clearly.

During my personal-issue time block, I made certain that I *only* dealt with personal issues. If work ideas arose or I received work texts or emails, I would simply jot them down to deal with them later and return to solving my personal problems. At the end of the time block, I also summarized any unresolved issues for the next day before transitioning into work mode or relaxation mode if the time block was at night. Likewise, if a personal issue arose during my work time block, I avoided dealing with it and simply wrote it down for my next personal time block. This way, I ensured that I was fully present and focused on both areas of my life!

Chew on This . . .

Try making this **Daily Bite of Time-Blocking** exercise a ritual to help transform your focus and balance, fostering a sense of intentionality in your daily life.

- **PORTION YOUR FOCUS:** Imagine your day as a menu. Choose one area of life (or course) to give your undivided attention to. What is worthy of your focus today? Is it your personal well-being, family, or work? At what time will this time block occur?

- **SET THE TABLE:** Create the ideal setting for your time block. Visualize your zone of focus as a beautifully set table. Find your favorite cafe, a walking trail, or a comfortable room and arrange it as if you're about to engage in something truly special.

- **SAVOR THE MOMENT:** When you're ready to begin, allow life's distractions to melt away and enjoy the act of focusing. If random thoughts try to pull you away, simply jot them down and gently come back to the present area of focus.

- **DIGEST YOUR PROGRESS:** As your time block ends, reflect on what you accomplished and what needs additional attention. Create a new menu for tomorrow to keep the momentum going.

- **ASSESS AND ADJUST:** Just like perfecting your recipe, refine your time-blocking approach. What worked and what didn't? Are mornings or evenings most effective? Were you able to block out distractions?

cherry on top
MASTERING FEEDBACK FOR WINNING RECIPES

Do not spend valuable time and energy fully fleshing out a concept until you intuitively feel that you have a winning concept. You must *first* develop a fully fleshed-out concept that aligns with *your unique vision* before giving it to others to test and offer their honest, straightforward feedback. Relevant experience is always more valuable than impressive credentials for providing useful and honest feedback. Be willing to release your product into the world once you've integrated relevant critiques and believe it's as good as possible, which won't be 100 percent perfect. Remember that perfection is a nice North Star—an inspiring guide but ultimately unattainable. However, *perfecting* is something you can continue doing your entire life. In PD speak, this is called engaging in continuous improvement!

part 2

SERVING YOUR RECIPE

Releasing Your Product or Service into the World

6

PRESENT YOUR RECIPE

Connecting Your Product or Service to Consumers

You have gathered your ingredients, simmered them to perfection, unveiled your chef's-kiss recipe, and used valuable feedback to refine it. Now, you're finally ready to present your creation to eager customers. It's time for your concept to make an impact. The challenge lies in connecting with those who are most enthusiastic about experiencing it.

Successfully distributing your product involves a very clear set of steps: clarifying your core values and foundational principles, preparing your recipe to present to customers, and understanding your target market. Additionally, you'll need to thoughtfully select your channels of distribution, market your recipe, continuously support your recipe and customer base, and assess the skills needed to assemble the team you need to execute your vision.

CLARIFYING YOUR CORE VALUES AND FOUNDATIONAL PRINCIPLES

Before presenting your recipe to the world, it's crucial to define your central tenets and nonnegotiable beliefs that will guide and support every aspect of it. Which principles are critical to the well-being of your recipe, your customers, your (future) employees, and your communities? What truly matters above all else? Your personal core principles are the heart of entrepreneurship and will help steer your daily actions and interactions toward authenticity and a clear, unwavering ethos. To establish these foundational principles, consider the following steps:

- Define your "reason for being"
- Identify your core values and principles
- Translate core principles and values into concrete action
- Create your guiding principles manifesto
- Share the manifesto with your team
- Revisit and refine over time

Define Your "Reason for Being"

Start by asking these key questions:

- What is the purpose of your product/service?
- How do you want customers to feel after experiencing your recipe?
- What lasting memory do you want to create?

These reflections will shape your *mission statement* and your *vision statement*. For a heart-centered venture, your mission and vision statements are the only compass you need to keep you grounded and guided on your tumultuous entrepreneurial journey. A mission statement defines the purpose and goals of your organization and illustrates how it serves its target market on a daily basis. A vision statement describes your ultimate aspirations for the venture and the impact you wish to have in the future.

To craft your mission statement, you will focus on what you do, the customers you serve, and how you deliver value to them. You should be concise, authentic, and actionable. To craft your vision statement, you will imagine the ideal vision you wish to ultimately achieve. It's essential to think grand, be uplifting, and align it with your mission. Your mission and vision are essential to knowing where you're ultimately headed, and they will become woven into your conscience and intuition. They will not only keep you on track but continually stoke the fire burning in your soul that gives you the fortitude to keep going when times get tough.

Each statement should be concise—no more than a single, evocative sentence. Example: at M&D, our mission statement was to [create playthings that] provide a launch pad to ignite imagination and a sense of wonder in all children so they can discover themselves, their passions, and their purpose. Our vision statement was to empower teachers, parents, and caregivers to take back childhood, nurturing resilient, independent, critical-thinking children through facilitating open-ended play. To establish these foundational principles, consider the following steps.

Identify Your Core Values and Principles

Outline the values that are nonnegotiable for your venture. These may include:

- A commitment to sustainability

- An innovative spirit
- Accessible pricing
- Exceptional customer care, such as swiftly responding to needs and concerns, standing behind your products, prioritizing relationship-building, and valuing feedback

Your values will be unique to your venture and should reflect what matters most to you. For example, at M&D, our core values included prioritizing customer satisfaction, being product-centric rather than marketing-centric, championing accessible pricing, embracing trial and error, and reflecting on and learning from failure.

Translate Core Principles and Values into Concrete Action

Your core principles must be actionable to shape your company ethos. For example, if you value accessible pricing, choose your materials and where you manufacture the product wisely by selecting low-cost manufacturing partners and developing a lean business that supports low margins. If you value sustainability, choose environmentally friendly materials and packaging while remaining in alignment with your budget and pricing goals. If you value customer feedback, make it a key part of your product development process, actively seeking input, funneling insights into iterative improvements, and establishing a robust customer service function to gather and channel user perspectives.

Create Your Guiding Principles Manifesto

Compile your mission statement, vision statement, core values, and actionable steps into a one-to-two-page document. This manifesto will reflect your company's ethos and serve as a roadmap for your team.

Share the Manifesto with Your Team

Host a town hall to introduce your guiding principles to your employees, sharing their derivation and importance. It is critical that every single person on the team is inspired by your ethos. Integrate these principles into new employee onboarding, print out physical copies for every team member to post, and display them in high-traffic workspace areas.

Revisit and Refine over Time

Treat these guiding principles as a living, breathing entity that evolves naturally based on new experiences and insights. Regularly revisit them to inform strategic decisions, continue to gather employee feedback, and adapt them as your venture matures. Embrace your manifesto's dynamic nature as a reflection of your company's ongoing journey.

Story Nugget

> As part of the onboarding process at both M&D and Lifelines, I've made it a priority to personally meet with each new employee to immerse them in the heart of our mission. During this time together, I seek to articulate how their specific role is directly tied to our larger purpose, illustrating how their unique contributions are essential to the realization of our shared vision. I want them to feel both connected and invested in what they are doing each day and know that they and their work are valued.
>
> This has been one of my favorite parts of my role. I love witnessing their expressions change from curiosity to pride as they begin to see their work as not just a job but an integral part of something that is meaningfully impacting lives. I want every single employee to recognize that we have a deeply authentic brand rooted in a genuine, personal story. Our mission is more than simply a tagline; it is a true reflection of who we are and what matters most to us.

If I can align an employee's heart with our mission and help them see how their daily actions contribute to our future, they can become inspired by a profound sense of belonging and meaning. This sense of connection, I believe, can not only elevate the caliber of their work but strengthen their commitment to staying at the company for the long term. We actually use the term "lifers" at M&D for those who are so invested in the mission that they have the highest likelihood of making a lifetime commitment to the company!

PREPARING YOUR RECIPE TO PRESENT TO CUSTOMERS

Before consumers can even determine whether or not they wish to purchase your recipe, you must craft a narrative that captures its essence and appeals to their hearts and minds. Follow these steps to craft an engaging presentation.

Create a Feature and Promise Sentence

Create a single evocative sentence that encapsulates the features and promise of your recipe. For example, the description for the Lifelines Scented Lava Gel Pens is "The enchanting symphony of scented ink and flowing lava bubbles engages your senses and soothes your mind."

Highlight Special Features

List the unique features that make your recipe special. For the lava pens, these include:

- Scented ink—each pen features a unique, invigorating scent

- Mesmerizing visual experience with lava bubbles that rise and fall

- Gel ink that delivers a smooth, buttery writing experience

Use Vivid, Sensory Language

Describe how your recipe engages all the senses. The more evocatively you bring the experience to life, the more consumers will be enticed to purchase it! For the Lifelines Cloud Diffuser, we say, "Enjoy breathtaking aroma that diffuses into a visually soothing mist."

- Touch on aspects like texture, visual appeal, taste, sound, or how it makes you feel

- Share positive stories of use cases, special pricing, or uniquely sourced materials

Create a Catchy Tagline

A memorable tagline will grab your customer's attention. Examples of Lifelines's taglines include:

- Stress Relief Doesn't Have to Be Stressful

- Makes Your Brain Go Ahh . . .

- Come to Your Senses . . .

Ensure a Memorable First Impression

Beautiful presentation matters—whether you have a recipe or a product. For a recipe, focus on the serving platter or plate on which your recipe is presented and the garnishes used to accent it—fresh herbs on top, a drizzle of olive oil, or a carved radish as a flourish. Ensure that you are able to deliver the same level of quality and visual appeal for each and every plate that leaves your kitchen. For a product, focus on your packaging and its ability to convey the essence of your brand and its origin and mission story. Ensure that your packaging is appealing enough to be instantly eye-catching and resonate with its target market.

Guarantee Consistency and High Standards
Deliver consistent quality day in and day out. For recipes, use an approved, plated dish for those on the prep line to mirror and adequately train the kitchen team to deliver a quality dish every single time. For products, ensure that your production team has a signed-off production sample and a clear checklist of quality details to hit. Clearly communicate your quality standards so they're consistently maintained, even when you're not looking.

By focusing on these foundational principles, your recipe will become more than just a meal or product. It will transform into an experience, a story, and a quality brand that deeply resonates with your target market.

UNDERSTANDING YOUR TARGET MARKET

To create a product that is widely enjoyed and adopted, you must define exactly whom you view as your ideal customers. Delineate their positives and negatives and determine your differentiating features, benefits, and value-generating characteristics. Your target market will grow out of your positioning decisions. Questions to ask include:

- Who is the ideal group of customers that your concept is targeting? This is your target market.

- What are their demographics, including their gender, age, income, and level of education? What are their lifestyles, values, primary concerns, hobbies, and leisure activities?

- How do they break down geographically? Is there a particular country, city, area, or population that you are targeting?

- Where do they choose to shop, how do they shop, how do they use products and services, and how much do they generally spend on products and services like yours?

- What tone and language are you using to reach your target market?

- What is your tagline to convey your mission to your target market?

- What is your visual identity to evoke the mission on your packaging and content? What sets your product apart from the competition? It may be helpful to create a chart listing and comparing your features and benefits to those of your competitors.

Once you define your target market, you can also determine how you would like to talk about your brand to better connect with your audience and build trust and recognition. (From here, you can further narrow down your target audience, which is a subgroup of your target market, to pitch to in marketing or advertising campaigns.)

Without clearly defining your target market, achieving long-term success will be significantly more challenging. Take the time to dig deep and get specific. This focus will help you craft consistent brand messaging, sustain your passion for the brand, reinforce consistent core values, and authentically engage with your end users. While failing to define your audience risks misinterpreting their needs and expectations, clarity empowers you to establish enduring connections and deliver meaningful value.

Story Nugget

Transcendent missions often emerge organically, shaped by life experiences and crystallizing moments of insight. Both

M&D and Lifelines are examples of missions born from personal challenges and observations. M&D was inspired by observing the shift in childhood from a time filled with freedom and creativity to one dominated by overscheduling and resume-building. In response, we created open-ended playthings designed to spark imagination, independence, and critical-thinking skills in children. Lifelines, on the other hand, emerged from my personal struggle to break free from rumination. I discovered that immersing my senses in delightful stimuli was the fastest way to interrupt the stress response, cultivating calm and joy. In response, we created well-being tools designed to disrupt that stress response and foster a sense of equanimity.

Forging a deep connection with our M&D customers—both end users and retailers—was key to cultivating mutual trust that stood the test of time. Customers consistently credited M&D's growth to our willingness to always listen to their feedback and make improvements based on those suggestions. This began with responding personally to every single letter I received and regularly calling customers to understand how we could better serve them. These honest conversations with end users not only forged many amazing friendships but became invaluable in shaping and refining our brand, which is something we continue to do today.

THOUGHTFULLY SELECTING YOUR CHANNELS OF DISTRIBUTION

There are various methods of getting your recipe into the hands of hungry customers, so it's critical to determine which distribution method is best for you. These include direct sales, online sales, and retail sales.

With direct sales, your recipe is sold directly to consumers without intermediaries. This can be done through a physical restaurant, food truck, farmers market stall, or pop-up shop in addition to online platforms or direct sales representatives and campaigns. This distribution method allows you to directly connect with your consumers, building a deep emotional connection with them and granting you immediate valuable feedback.

For online sales, your recipe is sold through online marketplaces, e-commerce websites (your own or others), subscription boxes, delivery apps for home delivery, or social media platforms. This distribution method allows you to reach a wide audience and sell directly to consumers without the need for physical stores.

In the retail channel, your product is sold at a wholesale price to existing retailers, who then sell it to consumers at suggested retail prices. You can partner with grocery stores, convenience stores, cafes, or specialty shops to sell prepackaged versions of your recipe. This distribution method enables you to tap into their multiple retail locations, customer base, marketing and merchandising platforms, and resources as they help you expose your brand to many more people than you would be able to reach alone.

In selecting the best distribution channel for your unique recipe, you'll need to consider your target market, your financial and human resources, and your goals. If personal engagement and immediate, real-time input are vital to refining your product, direct sales may be ideal. To achieve a wider reach with lower overhead costs, online sales may offer an incredible opportunity, although they may ultimately prove more expensive based on the need for paid customer acquisition and relevance-enhancing strategies. If scaling more quickly and leveraging existing retail spaces to reach a diverse customer base is your priority, partnering with retailers may be the way to go.

You don't need to limit yourself to any one method. Instead, you might explore a combination of strategies. At M&D, we initially focused on retail sales and later added online sales, a move that proved extremely effective. We started with selling our products through existing retailers until customer feedback made it clear that they also wanted the convenience of purchasing our products online. It is critical to stay aware of market changes and customer demands. Continuously evaluate your approach, objectively assess its results, and adapt as needed. By aligning your strategy with your vision, understanding your strengths, and addressing the needs of your target market, you can build a successful and sustainable distribution model.

MARKETING YOUR RECIPE

It takes a clear strategy with aggressive, targeted marketing (and often direct sales efforts) to get your product into consumers' hands. Often, and perhaps sadly, the most delicious or innovative products aren't necessarily the ones that become ubiquitous. Rather, the products that compel users to want to purchase them are the ones that gain mass distribution. Think about it: does Chick-fil-A have the absolute best food? Probably not, but their marketing campaigns are incredibly compelling, and they have lines around the block. Use the following methods to engage with the community and build brand awareness: customized marketing messages, engaging content, collaborations with influencers, advertising, local media and events, promotions, partnerships, word of mouth, branded spaces, and personalization.

A Full Serving of Practice

Here is a step-by-step process to implement engaging, memorable, cost-effective marketing strategies.

- **UNDERSTAND YOUR TARGET MARKET:** Research their unique values, characteristics, and preferences. Identify the demographics you wish to target and the social media platforms they use most frequently.

- **CREATE CUSTOMIZED MARKETING MESSAGES:** Utilize specific language, imagery, and references that resonate with your local audience. Feature local stories, issues, and events related to your brand to help forge an emotional connection.

- **CRAFT ENGAGING CONTENT:** Produce captivating video content, blog posts, and social media updates that highlight the ethos of your brand. Utilize existing platforms to showcase your content and attract customers. Experiment with live events to explain concepts or showcase products. I have engaged in many live events for Lifelines to explain our new concept of sensory immersion. You could also create personalized videos for influencers or specialty stores to post on their social media platforms. I make many personal videos for independent retailers, and it is highly appreciated and quite effective!

- **COLLABORATE WITH LOCAL BLOGGERS AND INFLUENCERS:** Identify local influencers or bloggers in your target market who have strong local followings and can help promote your brand. Offer exclusive discounts and access to their audiences, free samples for them and their families, or collaboration opportunities that create stickiness for their followers.

- **STRATEGICALLY INVEST IN ADVERTISING:** Focus on targeted advertising campaigns where results can be clearly measured. Start small with ads in places like event directories. Lifelines recently advertised in the directory for the biannual Atlanta Market. At least a dozen new retailers tracked us down based on that $1,000 ad, and all of them placed orders. We broke even on those very first orders. We also place a recurring ad on the back page of our local high school musical program. Thousands of people attend these shows and comment on our support, building goodwill and brand recognition. Amazon-sponsored ads have also been effective for us, and they are easy to grow as you see returns. Only invest in advertisements that align with your budget and goals and are ideally instantly measurable. Swiftly abandon them if they don't prove effective.

- **LEVERAGE LOCAL MEDIA:** Write op-eds or press releases about your brand's involvement in the community. Engage local newspapers, radio stations, and TV channels to cover your events or story.

- **PARTICIPATE IN LOCAL EVENTS:** Set up interactive displays, crafting tables, or play areas at community events, fairs, and festivals. Give away small items to create goodwill and connection. Host your own events, such as workshops, demonstrations, tastings, or open houses to engage directly with your audience.

- **OFFER ON-THE-SPOT PROMOTIONS:** Offer discounts and run special offers or promotions during events to build excitement and drive immediate sales. Remember the adage "A bird in the hand is worth two in the bush." While you have customers captive, ensure that they leave with your product or sign up for your service. Do whatever it takes to get the sale!

- **PARTNER WITH LOCAL ORGANIZATIONS:** Collaborate with local businesses, nonprofits, schools, clubs, or local associations to co-host events and increase visibility. Co-brand products or events or offer joint promotions to enhance your credibility and expand your reach to new customers.

- **CULTIVATE WORD-OF-MOUTH MARKETING:** Exceed customer expectations in taste, value, quality, or experience to inspire them to share their honest engagement with your product. Go above and beyond in all customer interactions, and ensure that your service is friendly, caring, responsive, and solution-oriented. Listen intently to your customers and do whatever you can to respond to their needs. Actively encourage satisfied customers to leave reviews or refer family and friends by offering them incentives to do so, like discounts, cashback, or special gifts for their support. Add personalized touches that surprise and delight your most loyal followers, such as responding to customer inquiries yourself to build trust, loyalty, and repeat business.

- **SHOWCASE TESTIMONIALS AND USER-GENERATED CONTENT:** Highlight positive customer experiences and user-generated content and endorsements through social media and other channels. Use genuine testimonials and endorsements to highlight the extent to which others love your product and brand, and encourage others to share their experiences as well.

- **CREATE BRANDED SPACES IN MAJOR RETAILERS:** Erect branded displays within high-traffic retail spaces to showcase your recipe, leveraging their employees and existing customer base to help merchandise and expand the reach of your concept. Design unique merchandising fixtures that share and elevate your brand and attract customers. Take advantage of the opportunity to utilize existing retail space whenever you can. Lifelines currently has two beautiful "stores within stores" at Macy's Herald Square and Indigo Bookstore in New Jersey.

- **TRACK AND ADJUST:** Continuously monitor the effectiveness of your tactics through engagement metrics and customer feedback. Refine your approach based on what resonates most with your audience, remaining flexible and creative to maximize your marketing impact.

CONTINUOUSLY SUPPORTING YOUR RECIPE AND CUSTOMER BASE

It's important to support your recipe and customer throughout the product's or service's entire life cycle. Prioritizing customers' input and putting them and their experience with your recipe *first* will be essential to the success of your business. However, many entrepreneurs do not even consider the customer in their business strategy and planning. You cannot create a recipe that consumers will be eager to devour if you don't clearly ask or care about their experience using it. Ask them to explain in detail what they like about your recipe and what they don't, and have them list the exact changes you should make to improve it. Additionally, determine what other recipes they would like you to make or other services they would like you to provide. Caring about what your customers think and asking for and integrating their feedback to continuously improve your recipe is critical to gain repeat business and build long-term trust and loyalty.

Extraordinary customer care is a long-term strategy that always pays off. This includes immediate follow-up on all consumer concerns or questions and is a basic building block of creating trust and long-term customer relationships, demonstrating that you appreciate and respect them. In fact, the more personal you can make these relationships, the better! Try to ensure that your customers have such a remarkable experience that they want to tell every single person they meet all about it. Most companies care much more about their product or service than the customer. Your goal should be to make each customer feel valued and happy, no matter what it takes! Continue collecting and prioritizing feedback from customers and altering your product as needed to keep raising the bar and meeting their preferences and expectations.

Story Nugget

At M&D, we knew that customer loyalty was the key to our future. From the launch of our very first product, we prominently displayed our toll-free 800 number on the back of our products, even though in the early days, that number rang on our home phone at all hours. We desperately wanted to connect with our customers and hear everything they had to say so we could continue enhancing our products. For three decades, we offered live customer care and free replacement pieces for all our puzzles, addressing the primary reason customers contacted us. If no pieces were available, we replaced the entire puzzle, even though it cost us roughly ten dollars per customer to do so. Many loyal customers ended up working for our company based on the positive way we handled their complaints and concerns!

Our only directive to the customer care team was to transform every caller into an enthusiastic advocate for our brand, converting any negative feedback, especially complaints, into positive experiences. We trained our staff to take full responsibility for product defects, immediately responding, "I'm sorry," rather than reacting defensively and blaming the customer. We also sent immediate replacement toys plus extra special treats to anyone who had a poor experience using our products. Making the customer happy at all costs was all that mattered.

One holiday, we air-shipped an entire order of products from our factory in China to Massachusetts to meet a customer deadline, even though it meant taking a significant financial loss. We simply couldn't let our buyer or her customers down.

Similarly, we always provided free demo products to retailers to help them showcase our products and let their customers experience them firsthand, ultimately driving sales. Most retailers ended up selling even the demo product!

At the New York Toy Fair, our largest trade show, we went out of our way to create a warm, welcoming space for retailers amidst the chaos of the overstimulating event. We wanted them to feel as if they were family being ushered into our home. We offered them free coat check, breakfast, lunch, drinks, snacks, and a comfortable seating area. Each evening, we hosted group dinners, where customers and salespeople could connect—fostering relationships among retailers and strengthening their bonds with our team. Many lifelong friendships were forged at these gatherings!

CRAFTING YOUR TEAM AND STORY TO BRING YOUR IDEA TO LIFE

Your next step is to evaluate the skills required and assemble the team members necessary to refine and serve your recipe. I often mentor entrepreneurs who have developed an incredible product but struggle to market and sell it effectively. Bringing your standout recipe to the world demands exceptional creative, financial, and storytelling skills as well as technical resources, especially in today's saturated digital marketplace. Many entrepreneurs struggle because their teams lack crucial skills or because some team members may be skilled in certain aspects of the business but lack the passion to give those areas their full attention. As a result, important areas might be neglected or shortchanged as they focus on what they take most pleasure in doing. No one is uniquely skilled in or passionate about every single area of their business. We all have strengths and weaknesses and finite hours in the day. Attempting to excel at everything will likely lead to falling short in all areas.

Being able to evocatively tell your story and, if necessary, secure funding to launch your novel recipe is essential to any entrepreneurial venture. A highly creative entrepreneur who lacks the storytelling ability to persuade others of the merits of their idea will end up frustrated, as it's unlikely their concept will make it to market. Many of the most innovative products don't ever see the light of day because their creators can't seem to cut through the clutter and access the financial support needed to bring them to consumers. Selling your idea includes the capacity to elevate and promote your concept by calling attention to its merits while expertly persuading consumers that they need to spend their hard-earned money purchasing it. However, the ability to storytell and communicate the mission and vision are elusive skills for many introverted founders. Confident, glib salespeople who can effortlessly engage retailers and don't take no for an answer are game changers and the difference between getting your recipe into the hands of consumers or having it grow mold and spoil.

At the conclusion of the first ten cohorts of M&D Entrepreneurs, we hosted a *Shark Tank* event at our home. I was always intrigued by how the most successful funding outcomes didn't always align with the most groundbreaking ideas. Instead, the ideas that garnered the most funding were often those that were presented most compellingly. It wasn't just the strength of the idea that mattered but how passionately and effectively it was communicated. Crafting a vivid and authentic narrative is crucial when inspiring others to invest in your product or embrace your vision. This is how you inspire belief in your vision and motivate others to want to take action and support you.

A Taste of Practice

Your practice to craft this compelling and sincere narrative may include these core strategies:

- **BEGINNING WITH YOUR "WHY"** by verbalizing the motivating purpose behind your visionary recipe. Detail the problem you are solving and why it matters to you, your market, and the world.

- **UTILIZING EVOCATIVE STORYTELLING** by sharing detailed, relatable, personal experiences that showcase the authentic journey behind the creation of your recipe. The more passionate and vulnerable you can be, the more you will create a genuine connection with your audience. I make my story completely personal and often become emotional in telling it.

- **CLEARLY ARTICULATING YOUR IMPACT AND REACH TO DATE** by highlighting the concrete results of your recipe touching others and what it aspires to achieve going forward. Share letters from customers, real-time data, or anecdotes to illustrate the value and potential of your mission.

- **SHOWING YOUR TARGET MARKET THEIR ROLE IN THE MISSION** by aligning your vision with the hopes and dreams of your target market customers. Help them visualize how their support contributes to meaningful impact.

- **COMMUNICATING AUTHENTICITY AND CONSISTENCY** by speaking from your heart and remaining true to your brand's core values. Authenticity is the key to building trust and making your story memorable.

A Full Serving of Practice

Articulating impact through tangible examples is a powerful way to inspire belief in your brand and vision. For my two brands, I created a repository of "impact-to-date" moments—a collection of meaningful milestones and achievements supported by concrete proof, such as letters, photos, certificates, or charts. What began as a personal scrapbook for reassurance during challenging times evolved into a strategic storytelling tool—my most effective method of persuading and inspiring others to believe in our brand.

I discovered that nothing builds trust like tangible facts and examples. Whenever I needed to make a case, whether it was convincing employees to join our team, persuading retailers to stock our innovative products, securing funding from investors, or inspiring customers to purchase our products and support our brand, I relied on these proof points. They helped me tell a compelling story of our achievements, instilling confidence in our future vision.

In my presentations, I included data on the number of products sold, glowing customer testimonials, descriptions of partnerships with respected organizations like the American Academy of Pediatrics, and prestigious awards, such as Vendor of the Year from major retailers. I paired these facts with emotionally compelling stories to craft an authentic narrative that appealed to logic, the senses, and the heart alike.

This approach transformed our progress into more than just a series of achievements. Instead, it painted a clear and inspiring vision of our journey and our opportunities ahead. By demonstrating the significance, scale, and potential of our work in an indisputable and compelling way, I was able to change behavior, drive action, and inspire belief.

Chew on This . . .

Try this **Mini-Morsels of Impact** exercise to leave your audience with a satisfying, digestible, and memorable taste of your impact that moves them to join your team, support your vision, or become a loyal customer.

- **SELECT YOUR SNACK:** Choose one impactful moment, achievement, or data point that best encapsulates your broader story. Keep it specifically focused on a single testimonial, milestone, or recognition.

- **FLAVOR-ENHANCE IT:** Pair your proof point with a brief yet compelling narrative that tugs on people's heartstrings. For example, include a note from someone whose life you transformed or illustrate how a key milestone highlights your mission in action.

- **PLATE AND SERVE IT:** Present your morsel in a concise and visually appealing manner:

  - Pair a compelling sentence with a striking visual. For example, you could pair a statement like "Take back childhood by spreading the wonder of open-ended play—one child at a time" with a beautiful photo of a child playing with a toy or a graph or chart to show how the message is spreading.

  - Pair a short anecdote with a tangible item, like a customer testimonial printed above a stylized product photo.

- **CLOSE WITH DESSERT:** End your bite with an inspiring takeaway or call to action. Here's an M&D example: "This is just the beginning. Imagine our impact when we create a Take Back Childhood movement and inspire millions of children with the wonder of open-ended play."

FILLING THE SLICES OF YOUR ENTREPRENEURIAL PIE

Most entrepreneurs don't begin their ventures with the self-awareness necessary to assess early on what skills they specifically bring to their venture and which skills they need to acquire from outside. It helps to do this by thinking about your venture as a popular restaurant item: a pie. Each slice of that pie represents a necessary role in your organization. Which pieces of the pie can you uniquely and expertly fill?

Many of the entrepreneurs I mentor are unsure of their "passients," which makes it extremely difficult for them to build strong, cohesive teams. As a result of this lack of self-awareness, entrepreneurs often end up hiring team members with similar skills, failing to introduce new perspectives or necessary expertise to their ventures. This often leads to disaster, as multiple individuals end up operating in the same slices of the pie, lacking autonomy and constantly second-guessing one another. Step back and reflect on the skills you most enjoy using and those with the greatest potential to drive the success of your venture. If you don't readily know your unique skills that will contribute to your venture, ask close family and friends to list your special talents and abilities.

The next step in this process is to determine which of your unique talents truly ignites your passion. Talent without passion leads to boredom and burnout, and passion without talent leads to poor performance and feelings of inadequacy. Start by listing the unique skills and talents you identified in the first step, then rank them by how much joy and enthusiasm you feel when engaging in them, from most to least. If you have the opportunity to focus on what you enjoy most, this list will serve as your guide.

Early on, when you are in the growth phase of your business, you won't yet possess the resources to hire a qualified employee to fill every essential slice of your pie. Founders and start-up employees typically fill multiple slices of their pie. But ultimately, trying to do everything yourself will put "too much on your plate" with limitations and exhaustion. However, as soon as you can fill those slices with people who are more skilled and passionate about those areas that aren't your core strengths, the better chance you will have of your venture succeeding. Without filling these pie slices, your company will lack strong leadership and direction in many facets of the business. In fact, 65 percent of business failures are due to personnel issues, specifically conflict among cofounders.[1]

If you lack resources to hire full-time employees to fill your pie slices, you also have the option of hiring hourly experts to help you perform necessary tasks that you may not be able to effectively handle yourself. Many entrepreneurs overlook legal, compliance, and major personnel and hiring issues that seem insignificant when the business is small but can have major long-term implications if they disregard them or do them improperly. In certain key areas, it is worth investing in a bona fide expert to ensure that you're on the right path. Doing so will save you much agony and expense down the road!

Story Nugget

> Doug has always taken responsibility for our financial, legal, and compliance matters. Early on, despite our limited financial resources, he was adamant about securing top-tier accounting, legal, testing, and insurance coverage to set our company up for long-term success. He conducted extensive research to find brilliant, savvy, yet affordable professionals—young, scrappy go-getters who guided us to focus on essential investments while avoiding common traps and unnecessary expenditures.
>
> Thirty-five years later, those same accountant, lawyer, and insurance agents are still by our side. As their experience has grown, so have their rates, but they've proven to be our wisest investments. Their expertise has helped us immeasurably, from negotiating agreements to helping us fight copyright infringements to setting up systems and safety nets that have protected and sustained us over the years.
>
> To maximize limited resources when building a team, it is critical to ask these foundational questions: 1) Do I have hiring

resources available? 2) What actions are necessary, and in what order of priority? 3) How can I allocate these limited resources most effectively? 4) What real-time data is essential for making critical decisions?

Do I Have Hiring Resources Available?

It's time to ask yourself, "What resources do I have available to hire a team, and how will I allocate those resources? Can I afford to hire experts to fill the slices of my pie?" Whether your answer to these questions is yes or no, let's look at how you can move forward from those responses.

YES, I CAN AFFORD TO HIRE OTHERS: With ample resources, you won't need to try to handle areas that aren't your natural "passients." Rather, you will hire "experts" who can perform tasks more efficiently and expertly than you. However, because entrepreneurs often believe they know their businesses best and are, therefore, best skilled to make every single decision, they tend to micromanage and want to control all areas of their operation. Many remain unable to delegate and attempt to do everything themselves when they aren't skilled in (or passionate about) all the critical areas of business. Even once they have filled their slices of the pie with skilled employees, some still don't let go of the reins and give their lieutenants autonomy to execute their roles.

NO, I CANNOT AFFORD TO HIRE OTHERS: Sometimes we must, due to limited resources, manage all areas of our venture ourselves for a certain period of time before the business has funds to support hiring others. If it all falls on you, how will you direct your valuable time? It's essential to value your time like shaved truffle and use it to maximize the areas that truly "bring home the bacon." For us, these have always been centered around creating extraordinary products and engaging in exceptional sales efforts to distribute those products.

PRIORITIZING KEY ACTIONS FOR ENTREPRENEURIAL SUCCESS

To successfully move your venture forward, it's crucial to identify and prioritize the most strategic steps necessary for sustainable growth. These steps, when properly executed, will ensure that your venture is set up for success and capable of overcoming challenges. They include hiring the right roles and investing in the right tools, the power of delegation and focus, essential roles for growth, effective training and communication, and securing emotional and cognitive support.

Hiring the Right Roles and Investing in the Right Tools

Establishing a clear hierarchy for hiring roles is essential as your resources grow. One key position to consider is a head of technology. In today's competitive environment, succeeding in the digital arena demands specialized expertise. Navigating platforms like Amazon or building a robust social media presence is nearly impossible without skilled professionals. Twenty-five years ago, we managed Amazon and social media completely on our own. However, with Lifelines, the rapid pace of digital change made it necessary for us to hire seasoned firms that specialized in these areas.

Constrained by limited resources, many of my M&D Entrepreneurs attempt to create their own logos, branding, and packaging. However, this often leads to subpar and unappealing results. What might have worked two decades ago, when no method existed to create and expose immediate feedback and reviews, is no longer sufficient, especially for premium products like beauty items. Allocating your budget to hire part-time brand architects and graphic designers, even one at a time, is a critical investment. Their expertise can significantly enhance your brand's impact and set you up for long-term success.

In addition to hiring the right team members, you will need to invest in tools, such as equipment and software, to distribute your recipe efficiently and effectively. It's critical to budget for these purchases so you don't run out of resources as they're needed. It's equally important to assess potential risks, like sales falling short of projections, the cost of raw materials rising, or new tariff implications. Evaluate how you can prepare for these risks in advance, and develop a contingency plan to minimize disruptions to your process.

The Power of Delegation and Focus

Knowing your "passients" and delegating everything else is critical to success and is one of the most important skills for managing your business effectively. It helps you protect your precious time, focus your energy on what matters most, and empower others so they can be efficient and best grow the organization. If you cannot relinquish your need to control everything and trust your competent employees, you most likely won't succeed in the long term because you will shortchange the areas where you *can* uniquely make a difference and best influence your venture's growth. Businesses generally start making money only once their founders offload the things they're not as good at and focus on the things they're best at, as that impacts the business most measurably.

Do you currently have the necessary team members to focus on and effectively build this venture? If not, whom do you need and in what order? How will you find them? What task will each employee be responsible for, and what are their specific job descriptions?

Essential Roles for Growth

Entrepreneurs often underestimate the number of administrative tasks necessary to run their venture, which ends up consuming a lot of time, especially as they grow. Bookkeeping, accounting, and customer care issues can easily comprise *three* full-time jobs and are all critical parts of building a successful business! Yet without key members on your team focusing on these areas, your business may falter.

Another necessary role is someone dedicated to managing the company's finances since inadequate management of cash flow will lead to instability and, ultimately, failure. Without sufficient funds available, your business won't be able to fund its daily operations, hire amazing team members, invest in exciting new ideas that can lead to growth, or manage unforeseen expenses. Managing limited financial resources takes a great deal of financial planning and budgeting. You must know exactly what's coming in, what's going out, and what you are projecting to need in the future. Given that budget needs and constraints change daily, someone needs to have their hands on that pulse every single day to help you prepare for what's around the bend and be ready for market changes. If you don't have clear visibility into your business and a flexible strategy for managing your cash and operations, you will struggle to navigate the inevitable challenges that come with growth.

Effective Training and Communication
Another time-consuming task that often gets neglected when you're trying to do everything yourself is properly training new employees. Many start-up employees are thrown into the fire without being given proper instructions for their role. Employees must undergo thorough training, completely understand all policies and procedures, and fully embrace the mission, vision, product, sales, and customer care strategy to successfully advocate for your product/service and effortlessly interact with customers. And then, it's critical to empower your team members by letting them own their decisions with a direct line of sight to you for advice and guidance.

Clear communication with everyone on the team is essential to build high morale and keep turnover low. While neglecting to train every employee in your mission and vision may seem like a time-saving measure in the short term, it ultimately risks dampening inspiration and motivation, resulting in long-term retention challenges. This also includes frequently recognizing the contributions of employees and showing them appreciation for their hard work, even if it's with a simple phone call or written note. Showing appreciation goes a long way in making employees feel valued, like what they do each day matters to the larger organization, and like they are an integral part of your mission!

Securing Emotional and Cognitive Support

There is one final, essential element to consider for your team: a critical support role that may not require a formal hire but is nonetheless invaluable. This role involves finding at least one person who can offer you both emotional and cognitive support throughout the challenging process of building your business and crafting your recipe for success. This individual will provide emotional reassurance during tough times and, ideally, possess a deep understanding of your field and products to provide informed advice. Your support system could come from a single advisor/mentor or be split among several personal friends or founder peers. It may also come from your business partner, as it did with Doug and me.

Securing a support system is crucial to staying grounded, maintaining your sanity, and navigating the journey effectively. Without it, you risk burnout and self-doubt, which can hinder progress and lead to setbacks. Seek out this special relationship early on, as it will be a lifeline throughout your entrepreneurial journey.

Story Nugget

> One of my college-aged daughters has a new venture that is just starting to generate revenue, but she is already becoming inundated with customer service issues and has proclaimed that she could use an entire team to help her handle them. She realizes that it is critical to manage all her customers' concerns quickly and efficiently, but if she personally ends up spending all her time doing so, she won't be able to brainstorm larger initiatives and conceive ways to build and grow her company. M&D has proven to be a good example for our daughter. For

the first few years, Doug and I handled everything—we even typed up invoices and packed and shipped every order to retail stores! However, these time-consuming tasks ultimately began impeding our ability to spend more time selling existing products and ideating new concepts. We decided it was time to hire an accounting and shipping clerk to allow us more time to spend selling our products to retailers. That was when we really began to take off.

Offloading mundane tasks for more impactful ones continued as we grew. I was selling full-time during the day and brainstorming products at night. But after thirteen years, that wasn't enough. I realized I needed to dedicate more time to creating rather than selling so I could develop additional products to expand our sales relationships. It was a very emotional experience giving up my retail accounts after over a decade of building relationships with them; however, we would be able to gain additional shelf space in those precious retailers only if we had many more products to offer them.

Given that I was the only one who could create new products and categories, but *not* the only one who could sell them, it was time to devote all my energy to product development. The truth was I wasn't the best salesperson, and there were many others with the passion and talent to develop strong relationships and sell those products to our retailers. Moving from full-time sales to full-time product development was a game changer for our company and a catalyst for explosive growth. In fact, the amazing person I entrusted to handle my treasured customers did a much better job than I ever did with them, growing those relationships to new heights!

A decade later, I experienced another turning point when I realized that I didn't truly enjoy the managerial responsibilities that came with being co-CEO. My passion was in product development, and I wanted to dedicate even more time to that and espousing the mission. To align my heart with my passion,

I ceded my co-CEO title solely to Doug and became chief creative officer (CCO) instead. The shift was transformative, enabling both of us to maximize our talents, improve our effectiveness, and find greater contentment in our roles!

Of course, my unhealthy ego didn't like ceding the CEO role and taking on the lesser role of CCO. However, by that point, I had become completely self-aware and needed to follow my heart, which was set on being authentic and engaging in what would best impact our company. Likewise, Doug thrived in the CEO role and was best equipped to help the company by further spreading his wings without me in his way.

Once Doug and I focused on our strengths, it facilitated a period of amazing growth. After twenty-five years, we were finally maximizing our impact on the organization. We also continued to evaluate and align other leaders' roles in our company to match their "passients" to areas of greatest impact. This led to more fulfilled individuals and greater organizational impact. And with Lifelines, we continued right where we left off, with Doug as CEO and me as CCO. They're the only roles we can authentically fill because they're the areas we're most passionate about and the ones where we can contribute the most. And we're truly enjoying every minute!

More than anything else, maximizing organizational impact takes becoming supremely self-aware. Each person must reflect on their personal strengths, weaknesses, and preferences to determine how they can best impact the company. By understanding their unique skills and what ignites their passion, they have the opportunity to adjust their roles and responsibilities to operate in a position where they excel. This role realignment not only increases individual satisfaction but helps maximize overall organizational efficiency and growth. Even if an immediate role adjustment isn't possible, understanding your "passients" allows you to proficiently evaluate your current position and plan strategically for the future.

What Real-Time Data Is Essential for Making Critical Decisions?

Accessing and analyzing data is the key to being able to effectively measure your venture's performance. If you don't have visibility into your real-time performance, it will dramatically limit your capacity to make educated, data-driven decisions. Without data, you are cooking with your eyes closed. Critically analyzing market data will also help you assess how the market is responding to your concepts and which recipes are selling and which are not. If you are a product company, a critical data point will be planning your inventory levels so you have enough of the strong sellers without overstocking the weak ones. Inventory management is key to achieving your sales objectives, and if planning ahead isn't a skill that you possess, you will need someone on your team to manage this.

More broadly, data helps you confirm whether your hypothesis was correct or not. And in both cases, why or why not? By analyzing real-time data, you can then determine which actions to take and when. What areas do you need to focus on more intently, and which do you need to improve, eliminate, or change altogether? Data allows a business, especially a small one that doesn't have to navigate lots of corporate layers, to be able to swiftly respond to what the market is saying.

Most fundamentally, you will need complete visibility into the revenue you are collecting and the expenses you are paying. It sounds basic, but you must ensure that your expenses don't exceed your revenue and that you are budgeting and allocating that revenue appropriately. The number-one reason small businesses fail is inadequate cash-flow management. In fact, the failure rate is 82 percent.[2] Insufficient funds can hinder your ability to manage day-to-day operations, maximize growth opportunities, and address unexpected challenges and expenses that arise. This could result in financial instability and eventual failure.

Early on, I struggled to fully embrace the power of data in shaping our product strategy. At times, I resisted what the numbers were telling me, relying instead on assumptions about how our products would succeed. Over time, I learned that ignoring data led to costly missteps, while leveraging it became the key to unlocking real growth. Here's how the shift unfolded:

NOT MAKING USE OF DATA: For our first decade in business, our M&D distribution strategy was to sell our products through independent specialty stores. While some retailers were passionate about understanding and joyfully educating customers about new products, most were unwilling to put in the hard work required. They said they wanted to do so, but in the end, they had too many other tasks, not enough seasoned help, and no energy or bandwidth to help push our products into the hands of consumers.

Many of my products were what I called "mysteries in a box," concepts that needed an investment of time and attention to explain their merits to customers. I *assumed* that our retailers would do whatever it took to convince their customers to purchase them, but in reality, they did not have the desire or bandwidth to do so. I didn't want to accept this truth or believe the data that clearly showed that these obscure products rarely generated an acceptable return on investment (ROI).

Because I resisted this objective truth, I found myself repeating the same mistake: launching innovative product lines with features that weren't immediately apparent through packaging alone. It took me well over a decade—and more failures than I care to admit—to realize that our product features needed to be crystal clear. We couldn't rely on retailers to communicate their value. Instead, our products and packaging needed to do the heavy lifting and sell themselves.

MAKING USE OF DATA: Evaluating market data is now a critical element of my product development process. At Lifelines, our initial product launch included introducing products across multiple categories, like essential oils, diffusers, and scented writing. The early selling data clearly indicated that our scented pens and pencils resonated much more deeply than other items and had gained especially strong traction. So strong, in fact, that it became clear we needed to immediately divert all our engineering and design resources from brand-new categories to creating a broader writing category. One year later, we are growing that segment based entirely on utilizing that early data. That's the only way to turn a couple of great-selling appetizers into an entire buffet before competitors get wind of it and find their way into your kitchen.

cherry on top
SERVING UP YOUR MASTERPIECE

Develop a deep understanding of your "passients" and identify how they uniquely position you to excel in your venture. Once you have the resources, concentrate on leveraging your strengths and delegating tasks that fall outside your expertise. Prioritize maximizing the quality and potential of your existing concepts by fully optimizing them before pursuing new ideas, producing more units, refining features or design, or offering variations. Ensure that the original version is refined before expanding. Next, remember that no matter the type of market data you analyze, even consumer insights from focus groups, you can never truly gauge a product's potential until it gets into the hands of actual consumers. Lastly, keep your creativity free and safe from undue pressure. Don't demand that your recipe "bring home the bacon" too soon. Allow it to flourish organically without forcing it to immediately support your existence!

7

FOOD FOR THOUGHT

Tackling Entrepreneurs' Most Pressing Concerns

We will put the finishing touch on our recipe by tackling another cooking adage: "If you can't take the heat, get out of the kitchen." In other words, if you cannot handle the pressure, challenges, or difficulties of a situation, you should immediately remove yourself from it. This concept originates directly from the idea that working in a hot kitchen requires extreme tolerance for heat and stress, and if you can't endure those conditions, you should step away. The very same can be said for entrepreneurship, suggesting that founders need to develop resilience and the capacity to handle stress in the challenges of the role or do something else altogether. However, had I heeded that advice, I wouldn't be an entrepreneur today. I surely would have succumbed to perfectionism, fear of failure, and continual impatience to arrive and chosen a career with much less "heat."

Learning to fight through the blazing inferno of bringing concepts to market and striving to get back up when scorched by that fire has been both the greatest challenge and greatest achievement of my life.

If you can learn to embrace the discomfort of that heat while remaining calm, cool, and collected, you'll develop the ability to harness something profound within yourself. Yet the entrepreneurial kitchen is never without its hazards—sharp objects, potential dangers, and the constant temptation to "hang up your apron."

To help navigate these challenges, I've compiled the most common burning questions I receive from mentees navigating "the pressure cooker" of entrepreneurship along with my candid responses. I hope my firsthand experience overcoming entrepreneurship's many trials will offer you the support and reassurance you need to keep going, even when the heat and pressure feel unbearable.

IS IT SUPPOSED TO BE THIS HARD?

Yes, it is absolutely supposed to be this hard, and thank goodness it is! That is why so few build successful entrepreneurial ventures and why those who do aren't immediately overtaken by competitors. Each challenge you overcome narrows the field, leaving fewer rivals snapping at your heels. Doug and I experienced this firsthand, facing an endless stream of hurdles. Every day felt like an uphill battle. We would conquer one obstacle only to encounter another, different in size and shape but equally daunting.

After about a decade, we had a realization: there would never be a year without major obstacles. So instead of worrying *if* we would face challenges, we accepted that we *would* face challenges and began expecting them. We then started saying, "I wonder *what* our distinct challenges will be this year?" This shift allowed us to approach obstacles with curiosity and resilience, using them to improve our products, strengthen our brand, and expand our learning.

There were times when we felt like we'd never overcome a particular setback, like needing to refund retailers for an entire shipment of damaged pretend-play kitchens due to inadequate packaging or discontinuing our entire Puzzle World line when it didn't sell and our customers demanded that we take it back. Yet we knew that being in business for the long term meant confronting every challenge head-on, even at a financial loss, since our mission was to make our customers happy *at any cost*.

Then one day, about fifteen years in, we looked up and realized something remarkable: those original competitors were no longer visible from our new vantage point, as we had achieved a scale where our new competitors were now household toy names like LEGO, Mattel, and Hasbro. But, of course, there was no time to bask in the glory of arriving since this inflection point presented a host of new challenges that loomed before us.

Over time, your challenges don't get any easier, but rather you gain confidence in your ability to overcome them. You begin to see challenges as a natural part of entrepreneurship and a catalyst for growth, wisdom, and longevity. Breaking conventions and creating groundbreaking concepts will always involve overcoming obstacles. But remember this: being knocked down is essential for growth. It separates the cream from the milk, and those who persevere not only move their ventures forward but also widen the gap between themselves and their competitors, making it impossible to ever be overtaken!

HOW DO I OVERCOME DECISION PARALYSIS?

Feeling overwhelmed by the sheer number of decisions required each day is entirely normal, and I've had to work hard to avoid falling into the trap of decision paralysis. One common cause is uncertainty over whether or not you're making the correct decision and coming to the "right" solution. This loop of repetitive thinking leads to endless second-guessing and a ruminative cycle that stalls progress. The ensuing anxiety prevents our mind from detaching from our ingredients long enough to let simmering occur and allow genuine solutions to emerge.

Much of this paralysis stems from "all-or-nothing" thinking, where every decision becomes too important and feels like it carries life-or-death consequences for your venture. I've had to reframe this belief, recognizing that no one decision defines success. If a choice turns out to be wrong, you can *always* make a new decision at the next juncture. You'll never have all the answers beforehand; decisions are made with the best information you have available at that moment. By making a decision and putting it into action, you will receive helpful new ingredients of information that enable you to learn more, become wiser, and more expertly make the next decision.

Through years of making one decision after another, I have learned that progress comes not from achieving perfection but from consistent action. Even if you take an occasional step backward, it is far preferable to keep moving in any direction than to remain stagnant, paralyzed by endless deliberation. You will always have the option to course-correct later.

Another life-changing habit has been breaking seemingly insurmountable tasks into bite-sized, achievable steps. Trying to attain your ultimate vision overnight, whether it's growing a multinational business or saving humanity, can leave you feeling incapacitated by expectations that are too lofty. Instead, stay in the moment and focus on small goals that you can accomplish today. These small wins are empowering and build confidence, moving you *gradually* toward that ultimate goal. This creates momentum to tackle bigger challenges over time. There is no rush. Focus on solving one problem at a time, and fix problems as they arise.

Engaging in action is the very foundation of progress, and humans are wired to continually evolve and progress. We are most fulfilled when we are accomplishing small but meaningful goals and feel a sense of accomplishment and empowerment. And, of course, engaging in those continual, bite-sized goals is critical to getting things done to move your venture forward *without* becoming overwhelmed.

Have you heard the expression "biting off more than you can chew"? When you focus solely on the mammoth end goal and try to swallow a huge task whole, you're likely to choke. But breaking a big task into manageable pieces allows you to digest it gradually. Most people give up before they finish, becoming overwhelmed by the enormity of the task. But by consistently completing small, daily goals, you'll keep progressing and move your venture forward. And one day, you'll lift your head and realize that you've outlasted all the rest.

Remember, this is not a race to a finish line. Arrival is the result of many years of incremental progress, one step at a time. As Douglas Horton wisely revealed, "Action cures fear, inaction creates terror." So keep taking action, no matter how small, and keep going. You've got this!

WHAT IF MY RECIPE HAS ALREADY BEEN INVENTED? CONVERSELY, WHAT IF IT'S BEFORE ITS TIME?

There are very few concepts that have never existed before in some form or fashion. Remember, "discovery consists of seeing what everyone has seen, but thinking what no one has thought."[1] It doesn't matter if the idea has been done before; it hasn't been done by *you*, with your unique blend of ingredients and distinct perspective.

By combining existing ideas with your authentic ingredients of life experience and personal interpretation, you can craft a recipe that's uniquely your own. This is the essence of authenticity versus originality, and *both* can be equally groundbreaking. Shift your focus from what has already been done to what you can singularly bring to it. Transform what exists with your perspective and lens on the world. Don't do it for others. This is *your* unique take on the concept or problem. Create for yourself, infusing the ideas you love with your honest voice and original point of view. True innovation with staying power is a genuine reflection of who you are.

I often mentor entrepreneurs who develop extremely creative concepts—so creative, in fact, that their target market finds them too avant-garde to fully embrace. If this sounds like your situation, you have three choices. Which one you select ultimately depends on what currently matters more to you: getting your concept into the hands of consumers or maintaining your exact vision without adjustments. First, you can stay true to your vision as is without any changes and slowly socialize it with the world, knowing that it may be before its time and not gain significant traction. Alternatively, you can seek concrete feedback from your target market and adjust your concept to better resonate with a broader audience. This is my preferred option, as my meaning is forged from getting the product into customers' hands. Lastly, you can let it keep simmering on a back burner, add salient ingredients, and reintroduce it at a later date, when either the recipe has improved or preferences have shifted. I will share an example of this option soon!

WHAT IF A COMPETITOR COPIES MY ONE BRILLIANT IDEA?

This is where our recipe for originality proves its true value. If you thoroughly embrace this process and let curiosity be your guide, you'll perpetually create innovative recipes throughout your life and will not have to worry about copycats. On the other hand, if your success comes from one lucky break rather than starting from scratch and letting curiosity guide the way to creative ideas, you may find yourself being terrified of copycats. Clinging to the success of that single concept instead of venturing back out into the world and pursuing new ideas limits your potential. Groundbreaking concepts are born from exploring and gathering ingredients of inspiration again and again.

The heart of entrepreneurial success lies in the ability to keep moving your venture forward, one recipe at a time. Then, no one will be able to replicate the speed at which you can create and bring new ideas to life. In my experience, it takes close to two years for a product to gain market relevance and attract copycats. This gives you plenty of time to conceive more inventive recipes, establish yourself as the market leader, and run miles ahead of your imitators. I often say, "Anyone can replicate one product, but few can replicate an entire category." While competitors may attempt to skim the cream off your line with relative ease, they cannot take the whole milk without tremendous effort. By continuously innovating and evolving, you'll remain the clear leader and ensure that your ideas remain the cream of the industry!

WHAT IF I CANNOT FIND AN IDEA I'M PASSIONATE ABOUT? OR WHAT IF I LOVE MY IDEA BUT IT'S NOT FINANCIALLY VIABLE?

Try not to rush finding that perfect idea or investing all your energy in a half-baked one. You have your entire life to gather ingredients, have crystallizing experiences (discussed in chapter 2), and discover the AOI that moves you to authentic action. Just let curiosity and an entrepreneurial mindset lead the way as you navigate each day.

In the meantime, consider joining a business that has a mission or cause that you genuinely believe in. We adopt children and pets whom we love dearly and that become our own . . . *why not a mission or a cause?* Our employees feel and talk as passionately about our mission as I do, if not more! Remain patient, engage in other vocations, and embrace other missions as your unique ingredients continue to simmer. That chef's-kiss recipe may take years, or even decades, of simmering to emerge, which is just fine! During that time, you'll be collecting additional ingredients and increasing the likelihood that transformative revelations will arise.

When that right idea finally sinks its teeth into you, be very deliberate about building it into an entrepreneurial venture. Forge your business gradually while working a regular job to pay the bills. Don't put undue pressure on yourself that your recipe must "put bread on the table" overnight. Creativity flourishes with extreme patience, not a rush mentality. There is no reason to leave your job unless your new venture can support you. Most good things take time. Savor the act of gathering, learning, and reveling in the process of creating something extraordinary. Ultimately, if your passion project doesn't become financially viable, cherish it as a meaningful hobby that brings you joy and fulfillment in your spare time. It doesn't have to be a business if it brings you joy and fulfillment. That's reason enough to pursue it!

HOW CAN I STAY STRONG WHEN I KEEP GETTING KNOCKED DOWN?

The key to staying strong amidst life's storms is building resilience—the ability to endure difficult times and emerge even stronger. Resilience enables you to bounce back from setbacks, adapt to change, and forge ahead despite challenges. Developing this skill requires *patience* and an investment in time to engage in continual practice like you would devote to honing any skill.

For me, enhancing this skill has mostly been a function of learning how to embrace failure through engaging in persistent trial and error and gradually easing up on harsh self-judgment. Over many years, I have finally adopted the mindset that failure is a necessary step on the pathway to success, helping you learn how to lift yourself back up, entrench your roots deep in the earth, and thrive. If you can accept the objective truth that all humans are fallible and make mistakes, you will have no choice but to become gentler with yourself and forgive your transgressions. Once you can more graciously allow missteps as a normal part of life, you will be better able to examine and analyze them honestly. They hold your greatest insights, growth, and wisdom and provide the recipe for improving your concept.

Most importantly, keep acting and taking those small steps every single day, even if some of them feel like they're moving you backward. Sometimes what feels like the lowest point is actually touching the edge of success, even though you may not be aware of it at the time. So keep pushing forward despite the heat of the kitchen and fight to get your recipes out into the world!

Since the road of entrepreneurship is so grueling, it is essential to connect with others who are experiencing similar challenges to understand that you're not alone. I would never have survived entrepreneurship without Doug by my side. Build a deep bench and support network—both emotional and cognitive. Talk with other founders, like those in the Inner MBA or other inspired founder groups, and form subgroups who meet regularly to share feelings, obstacles, and solutions. And most importantly, make certain that you take good physical care of your body and mind. I have worked myself into the ground at many points throughout my career, and it has been detrimental to me, my venture, and my family. Self-care and the ongoing effort to integrate work with play are essential for long-term life engagement and fulfillment.

Figuring out this satisfactory blend of work and play also provides a wonderful model to your employees, friends, and family members that it *is* possible to "have it all." Plan your days deliberately: schedule time for work, physical activity, family and friends, sleep, and hobbies. Without a clear plan, it's easy to let work consume you, which ultimately leads to exhaustion. By modeling equal measures of playful and purposeful activity, you will demonstrate to both yourself and others that you can give your utmost to your venture without burning out.

A Taste of Practice

A step-by-step practice to help build resilience may include finding more S.P.A.C.E. among our challenges, our feelings, and our responses! When faced with a dilemma, it's crucial to engage in the following:

- **STOP AND SENSE:** Stop and sense that you are now facing a challenge and could easily go into fight-or-flight mode and a stress response. Ground yourself by taking a few deep breaths, creating the SPACE to calmly respond.

- **PERCEIVE AND PIVOT:** Perceive exactly what emotions you are feeling. Then, pivot the situation by moving from asking "Why is this happening *to* me?" to "How is this experience happening *for* me? What can this experience teach me? How can it make me stronger?"

- **ADDRESS AND ACT:** Address the challenge by identifying one small action you can take. Breaking an overwhelming problem or situation into smaller, actionable tasks can make it much more manageable.

- **CARE AND CELEBRATE:** Offer yourself self-care by reminding yourself that everyone makes mistakes and faces challenges! Treat yourself with kindness, the same way you would a good friend, offering understanding instead of criticism. Then, celebrate even the small victories along the way, reflecting on how well you've overcome past and current challenges.

- **EMPATHIZE AND ENGAGE:** Empathize with yourself for being imperfectly and beautifully human, and make sure to engage in self-care and reflection as well as connection with others. It's essential to build a supportive network of friends, family, and colleagues for guidance and emotional support. Sharing your ideas, challenges, and feelings with others also helps reduce stress and opens you up to other perspectives. Also, take care of yourself by getting enough sleep, eating healthfully, exercising regularly, and engaging in mindfulness techniques to ease anxiety.

At the end of each week, reflect honestly on how you handled your challenging situations. Ask yourself, "What challenges did I face? How did I respond to them? What went well, what didn't, and how can I improve for next time?"

A Full Serving of Practice

Engaging in the S.P.A.C.E. practice time and time again has offered me two major life-changing by-products. The first is that I have learned how to let go of the things I cannot change and focus my energy on what I *can* influence. This has made me much more efficient and effective because I am able to home in on achievable goals, create a clear plan of tasks to act on, make meaningful progress toward achieving that plan, and feel an incredible sense of accomplishment that I am responsible and capable.

This practice of reflecting on my challenges also helped me solidify the second by-product: a growth mindset.[2] This involves viewing dilemmas as opportunities to gain more knowledge to learn and grow. The growth mindset also values patience and helped me to slow down and revel in the process. I realized that learning happens gradually and resilience is built painstakingly over many years of practice and persistence. By coming to believe that there was always something to learn, even from negative experiences, then developing the capacity to examine those experiences objectively and dispassionately to unearth those nuggets of wisdom, I was able to face life's obstacles with much greater confidence and adaptability.

Chew on This . . .

Try this **Stir, Then Savor** exercise to build resilience intentionally, one day at a time.

- **SAVOR THE MOMENT:** Start or end each day by spending a moment to taste exactly where you are. Consider both a current challenge and one recent positive experience. Notice how these moments made you feel without judging them; just notice the emotions they evoke.

- **MIX IN CURIOSITY:** Ask yourself, "What actions and attitudes (ingredients) are missing that could improve this situation? How can I 'spice up' this obstacle to make it more meaningful or appetizing?" Shift your perspective from "Why is this happening to me?" to "How can I learn and grow from this?"

- **PEEL BACK THE LAYERS:** Highlight one small manageable task (ingredient) to help address your challenge. Say it aloud or write it down and commit yourself to adding it to your pot today.

- **ALLOW SELF-CARE TO SIMMER:** Spend time nourishing yourself by enjoying a nutritious snack, taking a brief walk, or taking deep breaths to center yourself. Be patient, remembering that resilience takes time to grow and become savory like a slow-cooked stew.

- **TOAST TO YOUR SUCCESS:** At the close of each day, recount the steps you took, no matter how small. Recognize the progress you have made and celebrate your victories with those around you, like sharing a delicious meal.

IS IT NORMAL TO CONSTANTLY GRAPPLE WITH SELF-DOUBT AND IMPOSTER SYNDROME?

Of course it is! Self-doubt and imposter syndrome are very common, affecting individuals across all professions, skill levels, and life stages. High achievers frequently experience imposter syndrome because they always hold themselves to extremely high, and often unrealistic, standards. They may also doubt their inherent abilities, believing that their success is based on luck or external factors, leading to frequent feelings of self-doubt. Likewise, comparing oneself to others can amplify self-doubt. Developing self-esteem, confidence, and intuition can all help ease imposter syndrome. You cannot cultivate them overnight, but they are skills that can be greatly enhanced with practice.

A Taste of Practice

A few ways to help build self-esteem and confidence may include:

- **ENGAGING IN ACTIVITIES THAT LEAD TO A SENSE OF EMPOWERMENT.** Start small with things that you know you can accomplish effortlessly. Completing small, doable, bite-sized tasks, one at a time, will build courage, which leads to confidence. Biting off more than you can chew just leads to overwhelm. Slow and steady is the key to success. Moreover, try to focus on the effort you put in, not the outcome achieved. Realize that you don't need to change the world overnight.

- **LEARNING TO DEVELOP, TRUST, AND HONE YOUR INTUITION** through engaging in joy-filled, intrinsically motivated research on a self-chosen AOI that fascinates you. Amassing knowledge and experience in my AOI are key to my success and serve as essential, inimitable ingredients in every recipe. My confidence came from becoming an expert in my chosen AOIs, like creativity. Once we develop expertise, we come to recognize and appreciate how it sets us apart, which naturally boosts our confidence!

- **REALIZING THAT *HARD WORK ITSELF* CAN BE ANOTHER INGREDIENT IN YOUR SECRET SAUCE** and is a total game changer. Most people don't have the stamina to engage in grueling, repeated work day after day, year after year. Hard work always wins in the long run because while others are *watching* their lives unfold in front of them, entrepreneurs are *acting* and *engaging* in continual forward progress that propels them ahead of the crowd! Doug and I knew that a major ingredient in our success was our capacity to work harder than everyone else, day in and day out, for over three decades. And when we finally looked up, we were miles ahead of our peers!

- **IMMERSING YOURSELF IN LIFE** and engaging in as many life-changing experiences as possible. Gather more and more ingredients to form more unique recipes. More ingredients are the key to innovation and allow you to have more unique combinations and transformative recipes that consumers will be eager to devour. The fuller your pantry is, the more confident you'll feel knowing that you have everything within you to create innovative recipes! Once I trust that I'm housing all the necessary ingredients, I can relax and allow them to organically recombine into novel ideas.

- **STOP COMPARING!** Throughout my early life, I spent most of each day comparing myself to others and assessing where I was falling short. It was exhausting and a complete waste of my vital energy. But no longer! I now create concrete personal goals and continually measure my progress against them. I have also sworn off all social media, which only highlights unrealistic images that contribute to my feelings of inadequacy. And doing so has been life-changing for me!

- **FEELING THE FEAR AND DOING IT ANYWAY!** This is one of my favorite sayings and the title of a book by Dr. Susan Jeffers. Once you understand that experiencing fear is a necessary part of being human, you will realize that you can feel fear while *still* pursuing your goals. In fact, there is no way to face the unknown without experiencing fear. Refuse to be held back by *any* emotion, and continue to push forward despite the fear! Dale Carnegie once said,

"Do the thing you fear to do and keep on doing it . . . that is the quickest and surest way ever yet discovered to conquer fear."[3]

- **ACCEPTING AND ALLOWING YOUR FEELINGS.** These two words, "accept" and "allow," have changed my life more than any others. Instead of continuing to judge, deny, and repress my feelings, I have gradually learned how to accept and allow them. Although we are conditioned to never show the shadow side of our emotions, all humans experience their full gamut. There is no one who doesn't feel anger, shame, regret, bitterness, jealousy, guilt, despair, anxiety, or resentment. Once I stopped judging my authentic feelings, no matter how shameful they made me feel, I learned that they were a natural part of me and all humans. I gradually became more comfortable allowing them to flow through me without suppression and began to comprehend where they came from so I could reframe those flawed beliefs. Only then did they begin to ease.

    This exercise is still a vital part of my daily practice. Today, I am much more confident expressing, sharing, and harnessing the full range of my emotions, using them to be more creative and entrepreneurial. Find those true friends with whom you can express and share your authentic experience and feelings, and talk them out whenever you can!

- **HELPING OTHERS WHO ARE STRUGGLING.** I have found that supporting others allows me to feel empowered, feel that I have a purpose, and feel that I matter. This helps me gain confidence in my capacity to make a difference. When you help others, the gift is just as much yours. And that's not a cliché!

- **JOTTING DOWN YOUR NEGATIVE BELIEFS AND LEARNING HOW TO REFRAME YOUR INTERNAL DIALOGUE** to become more positive. This begins with self-awareness and noticing when you are being negative or self-critical. Once you notice the negative belief, take a deep breath, state it aloud, and say, "This is just a belief and not necessarily the truth." Then, ask yourself, "Do I have real facts to support this belief?" I then pretend that I'm a lawyer in a courtroom trying to use real evidence to contradict the false belief/claim of the prosecution. Basically, I am fighting to free myself from the negative mindset, offering as many current examples as I can find to support the actual truth. Then, I reframe that negative mind story to a more positive one. Instead of forcing it into an overly positive statement, I shift my perspective to one that is markedly improved but still authentic. For example, if I often berate myself by saying, "I never say the right thing," I may recall a few recent examples where I *did* say the right thing. Then, I'll change my negative belief to "There are times when I don't say the right thing, but there are also times when I do say the right thing. I am now becoming aware when I say the wrong thing and learning how to improve my responses."

These reframes help change my mindset from self-critique, shame, and punishment to curiosity, learning, and growth. You can also be your own cheering section, giving yourself empowering motivators, such as "I am capable of doing this! I can move forward, learn, grow, and become a better person." These affirmations will help you consciously believe in your capacity for change.

When you learn how to consciously reframe your thoughts, it's utterly transformative. My most common admonishment was "What is wrong with you, Melissa? How could you be so stupid?" This just made me feel even worse about myself. But now, my new mantra when I fall short is "Oh well, your intentions were good, you tried your best, and you're human. Let's learn from this and try not to make the same mistake again!" Although it sounded forced and phony the first few times I said it, I have now finally begun to believe it as pure truth!

A Full Serving of Practice

Learning to develop, trust, and hone your intuition is a lifelong journey that starts with immersing yourself in an AOI that sparks passion and joy—a topic that you are intrinsically motivated to explore. When you intensely engage with your AOI and build your expertise, it builds a strong sense of inner confidence. This knowledge becomes your hidden superpower because when you understand a topic at a deep level, it gives you the capacity to see it from perspectives that others may miss.

In my entrepreneurial journey, that AOI was wooden toys. I spent months in a New York City library researching the history, design, craftsmanship, and cultural significance of wooden toys throughout the world. My curiosity was insatiable, and my desire to learn more became an obsession. I didn't just read about wooden toys; I immersed myself in every possible aspect of this category. I discovered the evolution of these toys, the play patterns they were based on, and the craftsmanship that went into them. The more I dug in, the more I understood my connection to this AOI, as it became a personal mission to understand it better than anyone else. This wasn't about creating a new business; it was an entirely personal exploration of the progression and advancement of wooden toys throughout history.

This deep dive into my AOI made me more than knowledgeable; it made me a total expert. After a few intense months, I recognized that I probably cared more about and understood wooden toys better than anyone else. It was then that I could intuit what had worked, what didn't work, and what could be improved. This expertise gave me confidence, both in the category of wooden toys and in my own abilities. Through my personal dedication and passion for learning, I felt confident that I had a unique perspective to offer.

Through the process of developing expertise in an AOI, you'll come to see how it makes you special and sets you apart from others. This unique perspective will become your signature ingredient, enabling you to make more informed decisions, find solutions where others see nothing at all, and bring your distinct point of view to whatever you do. That confidence, born out of mastery over your AOI, will then spill over into every aspect of your life, allowing you to be more innovative, creative, and able to transform what exists wherever you go.

Chew on This . . .

Try this **Feed Your Expertise** exercise to identify and explore an AOI, one bite at a time!

- **SELECT YOUR INGREDIENT:** Identify an AOI that tantalizes your mind and palate. This is the topic in which you want to become a master chef. It could be as broad as "climate change" or as specific as "the history of wooden toys."

- **TAKE ONE BITE A DAY:** Commit fifteen to twenty minutes each day to tasting your chosen ingredient. You can:

    - Read an article

    - Watch a YouTube video, documentary, or online class

    - Practice a specific skill related to your AOI

- Connect your ingredient to other areas of life or work
- **DIGEST ONE INSIGHT:** After your daily bite, consider what you tasted. Extract one key takeaway or question you'd like to further explore. This spices up your knowledge base.
- **SHARE AND SAVOR THE FLAVOR:** Bring your ingredient to life by either sharing its goodness with others or applying it practically. Talk about it with other foodies, utilize it in a project, and brainstorm innovative ideas sparked by your insights. Sharing makes the dish even more savory!
- **PLATE IT WEEKLY:** At the conclusion of each week, reflect on your notes and serve up your progress. Recognize how the flavors are melding together to enhance your expertise. Celebrate your learnings and the knowledge base you're building!

HOW CAN I HANDLE THE PRESSURE TO ACHIEVE RAPID PROFITABILITY TO APPEAL TO POTENTIAL INVESTORS?

I continually see the urgency to achieve rapid profitability drive entrepreneurs' behavior. This pressure can significantly impact your business's long-term viability, leading to impulsive actions or decisions, such as refraining from incorporating beneficial features into your concept to maintain higher profit margins. Unfortunately, these unilateral decisions prioritize short-term gains and can ultimately harm your recipe, often causing irreparable damage. Your failure to consider the long-term implications of hasty financial decisions diminishes your willingness to take risks and explore innovative opportunities that could yield substantial rewards in the future. Essentially, prioritizing short-term gains will deter you from making decisions that could benefit your venture in the long run, despite lacking immediate returns. In fact, it's sometimes *more* beneficial for a business to initially operate at break-even levels and direct resources toward nurturing a robust customer base and securing market share for long-term sustainability. Not every business requires immediate profitability, and deliberately delaying it until the recipe gains traction and generates significant consumer demand can prove to be an astute strategy.

However, many entrepreneurs become incredibly excited about raising money and increasing their "valuation." It's a very ego-driven process, and how they value themselves and their business becomes a major form of competition and validation. Yet in truth, raising money isn't as romantic as it may seem. Investors have an obligation to give their clients a healthy return, and they need to honor that to maintain their credibility. So when you take on an investor, you will, by definition, be focusing more on profitability than other areas of the business that are critical to your success.

Raising money for a business is a complex process, fraught with challenges. It takes a great deal of astute mentorship to determine whether or not you need an investor and, if so, how to engage in proper due diligence and find the right partner who will honor your vision and support your growth. Steer clear of investors who put so much pressure on achieving a rapid ROI that it hurts your long-term business. I often see misalignment between founders and investors in not having a clear understanding of what exactly they are seeking in terms of ROI and the timing of achieving it.

I've witnessed many cases of businesses growing steadily but still not being able to satiate the appetite of the investor for swifter and higher returns. And then, depending on the capital structure and who has control, one of three things may happen: the investor may suddenly pull their money altogether, refuse to invest more, or replace you with a corporate professional who they believe can better run the business to achieve the rapid growth they seek.

I advise my mentees to wait as long as possible before taking money from strangers who prioritize returns. Investing in the right areas to build long-term brand value is often more beneficial for your business than focusing on immediate profitability, although this approach often conflicts with investors who prioritize short-term financial returns. Given that investors need to make a healthy return on their investment, raising money will put pressure on your venture to make a profit, perhaps sooner than it should.

Unless you have ample financial resources to self-finance, keep your day job to give yourself financial security and stability until your idea organically grows and allows you to step away financially. Before "putting all your eggs in one basket," investing your entire life savings, and fully committing to your idea, it's wise to first test it on a smaller scale. Otherwise, the pressure to achieve immediate success may compel rushed decisions, leading to the premature introduction of half-baked ideas. Maintaining financial security lessens fear, which provides the freedom to explore more innovative avenues and take calculated risks. It's always advisable to avoid "betting the whole farm on one crop" and instead strike a careful balance between your entrepreneurial ambition and financial stability.

I worked another job for a year when we first started M&D to help pay our expenses. I did it again when we ran into a business issue that impacted our revenue years later. If you rush to achieve profitability to satisfy an investor, you may cheat yourself out of creating anything magical. You won't have time to allow for simmering and will be creating completely out of consciousness. This can only spawn me-too brands with packaging alone as their differentiator and no real product innovation. And then, when you must raise money, go to friends and family first or get a credit line or bank loan before going to venture capital or private equity investors. That is, unless your primary mission is to cash out, which, of course, is counter to the heart of entrepreneurship!

HOW CAN I PURSUE MY ENTREPRENEURSHIP DREAM WHEN MY PARENTS AND/OR PARTNER ARE FEARFUL ABOUT FINANCIAL STABILITY AND WANT ME TO GET A "REAL JOB"?

It's important to first depersonalize others' comments and realize that those who care about us often voice concerns out of fear rather than a critique of our ideas. Humans crave security, and we naturally want to protect ourselves and our loved ones/children. Thus, we fear situations where our or others' safety is in jeopardy. When our family members or partners voice their concerns, it's often their fear speaking, not their lack of support or desire for our happiness.

To help alleviate their worries and ensure that their anxiety doesn't become your own and stifle creativity, adopt a slow and deliberate approach. Start small and build your business slowly and cautiously, adding one ingredient at a time and cooking a small batch before hosting a feast. Keep your day job while you craft your concoction on weekends, and in your free time, build a solid foundation that no one can doubt or question. Prove to your loved ones (and yourself!) that you are completely capable of doing this responsibly and maturely and that they have nothing to worry about!

That being said, sometimes your loved ones may remain fearful about you facing an unstable future, and no amount of reassurance can ease their discomfort. In such cases, acknowledge their concerns while assuring them that you have carefully evaluated your plan and are prepared for its challenges. Ultimately, despite their fears, stand firm that you need to follow what resonates in your heart.

My parents were not at all comfortable with my decision to quit my prestigious investment banking job, pool my meager life savings with my boyfriend, and start a toy company at age twenty-two. But despite their vocal worries that we wouldn't succeed, we did it anyway, and I am thankful for that decision every single day. Even if others don't fully support or understand your choice, your conviction and commitment to your vision will be enough to drive you forward.

You are ultimately responsible for creating your own path to meaning. Living authentically and pursuing your heart's calling is essential, even if it means stepping away from more traditional or secure paths. Today, my parents boast that their daughter and son-in-law have "made it," illustrating that their past worries came solely from a place of fear and concern for our future—not from doubts about the merits of our venture!

HOW CAN I REGAIN MY MOTIVATION AND AVOID BECOMING COMPLACENT AFTER A FEW EARLY SUCCESSES?

This sentiment is quite common! Once they achieve success, entrepreneurs often begin to feel too secure and fall into comfortable patterns, which causes them to remain stagnant and stop growing and innovating. When things are going well, we don't want to change anything, believing "If it ain't broke, don't fix it!" Humans unfortunately associate taking risks with danger or potential failure and the ensuing embarrassment. We are wired to remain stable and conserve energy; thus, we will naturally repeat existing routines since our bodies reinforce that we should stay safe and avoid seeking new data or attempting a new routine. In fact, the more consistent our past successes, the less motivated we will be to seek new ideas or address new problems promptly.

However, you are at risk of being swallowed if you don't continue pushing boundaries and advancing your venture. You must remain curious, learn, and grow in your AOI, or it will evolve beyond you and leave you behind. Continue expanding your experience and knowledge, not because you must but because it becomes autotelic and you intrinsically want to as an end in itself. Accepting the status quo, falling into autopilot, and never asking "why" has a dampening effect on learning, leading you to no longer feel the need to change or experiment. So you must fight your tendency to remain stagnant, continually try new things, and engage in new experiences to collect additional ingredients and keep your concepts fresh and vibrant.

A common example of this risk-averse behavior occurred with many of our independent retailers. They simply refused to adapt to modern technology when their customers were shifting to personalization, convenience, and seamless shopping experiences. Even these small retailers needed to become omnichannel and adopt sophisticated point-of-sale systems, or they risked becoming obsolete! However, they often stuck their heads in the sand and didn't stay aware of the latest trends to help them continually improve their business operations.

Since so many consumers are now turning to the internet for shopping and product research, a strong online presence isn't just beneficial; it's essential. It's also crucial for retailers to utilize data analytics that offer valuable insights into customer behavior. This enables personalized marketing and sales strategies, along with efficient inventory management.

Over our three decades, we also witnessed many toy retailers choose to stop attending the largest industry trade show, the New York Toy Fair. Instead, they elected to have their manufacturers' reps travel to their stores to show them new products. There were *so many valuable insights* to gain from that show—through networking, sensing the mood that season, visualizing trends, receiving show specials, talking directly to manufacturers, communicating to their customers that they traveled far and wide to discover the best new products—benefits that extended well beyond the relatively small investment to attend. Yet many retailers were content with remaining on the sidelines rather than committing themselves to growing and energizing themselves with new ideas to better serve their customers.

WHEN WILL I KNOW IT'S TIME TO GO ALL IN ON MY VENTURE?

You will know that it's the right time to go all in on your venture when your desire to jump in headfirst outweighs your fear of potentially failing. Moreover, as you learn increasingly more about your AOI, your passion for it will either shrink or grow. When your passion for bringing your recipe to fruition is *so great* that it has become an obsession with no easing up, there will be no choice but to get cooking, as you will be impelled from within.

I coined a mash-up word to describe the two opposing emotions present in stepping into the unknown and creating or trying something new: *exhilifying*. It is a combination of "exhilarating" and "terrifying." If the terror exceeds the exhilaration, you will become paralyzed and be unable to do anything at all—completely overwhelmed by the fear. However, if the exhilaration outweighs the fear, even slightly, you will find the motivation to take the leap despite still feeling apprehensive. To do anything groundbreaking and of personal significance, you *must* be in that space of both these dichotomous feelings and push against your comfort zone to "live life exhilified."

So my answer is always "If you're questioning your next step to such an extent that your terror exceeds your exhilaration, it's not yet time." Maintain the security of a job while continuing to gather ingredients in your spare time until the balance of those feelings changes. And if your feelings don't change, remain content with keeping your AOI a fulfilling hobby that is intrinsically rewarding and brings you joy.

WHY DO I ALWAYS WANT TO QUIT WHEN I HIT A STUMBLING BLOCK?

Perhaps your initial recipe hasn't found resonance, so you have become discouraged and stopped engaging in the hard work necessary to alter it to better serve the needs of real-world consumers and bring it to completion. This is where many ideas with potential are abandoned altogether, or entrepreneurs neglect the evaluation process and introduce a half-baked concept. It's commonly cited that a significant portion of people do not complete what they set out to do and struggle to follow through on their intentions. Why does this occur?

Humans Have Insecurities

While it may seem that most people have their act together, deep down, everyone is insecure about something. In fact, insecurity is a universal human experience. Some people might be more readily willing to admit to their feelings of inadequacy or unsure footing, but a sense of uncertainty or inadequacy does not discriminate and can affect everyone. For some, these feelings come gently in the form of quiet doubt, and for others, they hit as hard as a tidal wave.

Insecurity stems from comparing yourself to others. When you stop being okay with who you genuinely are and look outside at what others are doing, believing you need to be different to be accepted, insecurity creeps in. It comes from your healthy ego that is looking out for threats and trying to protect you from perishing or faltering, but it can also make you overly consumed with keeping up with everyone else, become unhealthy, and lead you astray. Overall, insecurity can undermine resilience, confidence, and perseverance, making it more likely that you will abandon ideas and quit prematurely, convinced that you lack what it takes to see them through.

We Erroneously Believe We Don't Have What It Takes

Because one idea rarely leads to success, we need a large quantity of ideas to access quality ideas. It is a little-known objective fact that entrepreneurs need to have lots of bad ideas to have lots of good ideas.[4] In essence, we need to fail more to succeed more. I have only given one speech that ever received a standing ovation, which was the one entitled "I Failed to Succeed," where I talked exclusively about my many failures. How ironic that personal failure was the topic that resonated most with others!

Dean Simonton, a brilliant researcher of intelligence, creativity, talent, and genius, states that the number of good creative ideas is a function of the total number of ideas, whether ultimately deemed creative or noncreative. Therefore, the odds that your one idea will be creative and break through the clutter are low. So if we have more ideas, there is a higher likelihood of some of them being good ones. Simonton says the only way creatives maximize the odds of creating a masterpiece is to produce a large number of ideas. Creative geniuses aren't qualitatively better in their fields than their peers; they just simply produce a greater volume of work, which gives them more variation and a higher chance of originality. The odds of producing an influential or successful idea are a positive function of the total number of ideas generated. His advice? Do a huge volume of work since quantity is the most predictable path to quality. The equal-odds rule, which distinguishes eminent creators, is based on the overall volume of ideas they have/works they produce. By sheer function of their productivity, those who reach professional eminence stack the odds in their favor of producing another masterpiece.[5]

However, James Clear adds that recent research has revealed that the equal-odds rule doesn't quite tell the entire story. It shows that deliberate practice matters and that you can improve your skills as time goes on. And as your skills improve, so do your odds of success. In other words, the odds of producing something good start to shift in your favor as your skills improve.[6] However, you still need to embrace the equal-odds rule because the only way to improve your skills through deliberate practice is to go through the volume of work. The result is still the same, which is to keep practicing and producing more and more throughout your entire life!

We Believe That One Failure Means We'll Never Be Successful Again

We often fall into "all-or-nothing" thinking, but in truth, it's impossible to predict how likely something is to be a success. Dean Simonton explains,

> It's a numbers game, and because you cannot predict success, the best strategy is to produce as much work as possible, which will offer more opportunities to hit the mark and create something meaningful. Selection processes operate on various levels, so the variation procedure at the cognitive level can't predict how a specific conceptual combination will be received. Even if a creator has a sound notion about what kind of product is most likely to get published or performed, they must be less confident about the long-term impact of that offering. As values shift, novel technologies emerge, or new facts appear—what

was once a success may later become a failure, and what is once ignored may later become belatedly acclaimed. In the long run, creators must lack foresight regarding the sociocultural merits of their ideas. If it were otherwise, we would have to consider creators a special class of prophets.[7]

So . . . if you want to produce creative ideas, produce as many ideas as possible! Don't think about the result; just keep creating. Some of those concepts will be original and practical, some will be horrible, and others will be average. It doesn't matter; just keep creating!

WHAT DATA OR METHODS CAN I USE TO BETTER GUARANTEE THE SUCCESS OF MY CONCEPT?

It's likely that every founder has dreamed of discovering that elusive recipe that would provide a clear, step-by-step path to product success. Because it would surely save us many years of blood, sweat, and tears! And there are scores of consultants and strategists who will claim to help you better achieve that success, using their well-honed "plug-and-play" models (these are systems that simply plug into what you're already doing and are ready to work the moment they're connected without any setup or customization).

We fell into this very trap at M&D. A former consultant on our team calculated that my new product launches had a success rate of just 38 percent, meaning that I failed more often than I succeeded. He was appalled and resolved to improve my success percentage to enhance our company's performance. His method followed the "plug-and-play" model of taking fewer, bigger bets on product launches and using more market data and consumer focus groups to ensure that those limited launches had a higher chance of gaining traction.

New Product Performance

Although some are great hits, my success rate is below 40 percent.

	2014	2015	2016 YTD
ITEMS LAUNCHED	176	230	67
STRONG PERFORMERS	66 (38%)	87 (38%)	17 (25%)
POOR PERFORMERS	110 (62%)	143 (62%)	50 (75%)

This strategy didn't sit well with me, as it ran counter to the approach I had relied on for over two decades. While most traditional consumer goods companies face high costs when launching new products, we operated differently. We were able to introduce new products incredibly cost-effectively and order them in small quantities. My tried-and-true method was to introduce up to three hundred new products a year in small quantities, quickly assess their market resonance, move forward with the winners, and discontinue the losers. This method had worked well, keeping our company profitable and growing steadily for twenty-five consecutive years. While I recognized that faster growth was surely possible, I firmly believed that the consultant's conventional method was a clear recipe for failure.

The truth is *no one* can predict the success of products or categories that haven't before existed, and consumers really have no idea what they'll love using until they are using it! Henry Ford has been credited with saying, or at least thinking, "If I had asked people what they wanted, they would have said *faster horses* [not cars]!"[8] The only way you can ever really know success is to get your concepts into the hands of consumers first, then honestly assess their feedback. Depending on a few selected launches puts too many eggs in one basket and is a much riskier strategy.

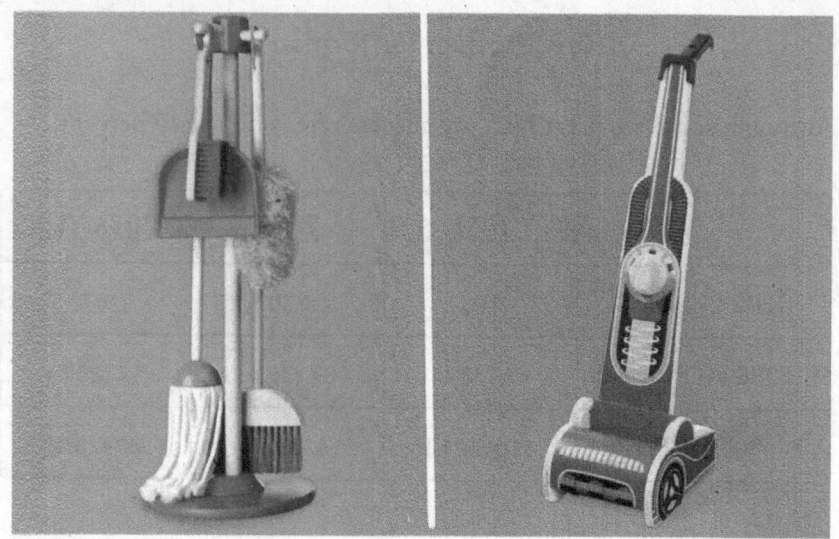

Melissa & Doug Pretend Play Sets: Dust, Sweep, Mop (bestseller) versus Vacuum Cleaner (poor seller and discontinued).

Both my own intuition and that of my team on product market fit are often incorrect and evolve with consumer feedback. For example, we introduced both a pretend vacuum cleaner play set and a broom, mop, and dust set called Dust, Sweep, Mop. No one on our team thought Dust, Sweep, Mop would "clean up" nearly as well as the vacuum cleaner. But in the end, it became our best-selling item of all time, spawning an entire cleaning category, whereas the vacuum cleaner never took off and was swiftly discontinued. This clearly proved once again that we never really know market resonance until the recipe has been served and tasted by your target market consumers.

As we touched upon in a prior question, there is another complex factor that determines whether an idea achieves acceptance, which is the timing of when it's introduced. Sometimes your idea might be amazing, but it has been put into the market before its time. Therefore, you may not know the ultimate result of an idea, perhaps for decades! Two personal examples of this are our wooden baby line

Melissa & Doug Cutting Salad Set (first prototype rejected in 2008 at New York Toy Fair).

Melissa & Doug Cutting Salad Set (enhanced a decade later in 2018, became a bestseller).

and our cutting salad food set. It took us three tries to succeed with the wooden baby line because we were too early; preceded the natural, wooden, organic trend; and needed some aesthetic improvements to make it look fresher and more appealing.

The cutting salad set came with vegetables that could be cut apart with a wooden knife. We brought our only prototype to the 2008 New York Toy Fair, but it didn't generate enough interest for us to produce it. Part of the reason for its lack of resonance was that salads weren't popular food items at that time. So our sole sample was placed on the back shelf of my office (my physical pantry!), which had become the land of misfit toys, displaying hundreds of my favorite failures. And there the salad set sat, literally imploring me to give it a second chance and bring it back to life (thank goodness it was made of wood, or it would have spoiled!). Ten years later, in 2018, salads were suddenly all the rage; we reintroduced that set, enhanced with kale and organic spinach, and it quickly took off, becoming one of our top twenty-five items that year! It is still one of our bestsellers today!

In this case, it wasn't a matter of success or failure; it was simply a matter of our *timing* being too early and *preceding* the trend! That's why you need to have numerous ideas. Because sometimes, it just might take a decade for the idea to gain support based simply on timing. In other instances, it may be that a minor aspect of your idea needs to be changed like price point, packaging, colors, materials, finishes, or instructions. It's never as black-and-white as either total success or total failure.

Lastly, sometimes the ecosystem might not yet be ready to support your innovation, and you need to wait until it's further refined. An example of this is electric cars, which were introduced in the 1990s but failed to take off because there was limited charging infrastructure, short battery life, and not enough public interest. However, today, with widespread charging stations, enhanced battery technology, and significant government incentives, electric car companies have thrived. This is timing at play once again!

HOW DO I NOT BECOME PARALYZED BY CRITICISM AND FEAR OF FAILURE?

Being an entrepreneur involves taking continual risks and failing repeatedly. You will, therefore, always face criticism. In fact, nothing you ever do will be beyond criticism. Therefore, as I mentioned earlier, you will need to continually lower the stakes of each decision in the current moment. You must learn to view your current performance in the context of millions of future decisions and the rest of your life. No one moment should become so high stakes.[9] Essentially, this concept teaches us to avoid overemphasizing the significance of individual events or decisions, realizing that they are part of a much larger continuum of experiences. This perspective helps us manage stress and maintain a balanced view of performance and outcomes.

To restate: the only way you will make progress and have a chance at success is to continually make decisions and engage in action. However, if each decision carries less weight and its consequences feel less dire, you can make decisions without fearing where they might lead. This is because you'll realize that new decisions will always come up as you gather new ingredients and information along the road, giving you the opportunity to adjust and make new choices. This approach is key to both staying sane *and* moving your venture forward. From *just one conversation* with a mentee, I can often tell whether their venture has the potential to succeed or not, strictly based on how they approach decision-making. Paralysis from over-analysis is *not* conducive to transformative thinking and successful entrepreneurship!

My other life-changing practice has been to develop a more positive mindset. What you think creates your beliefs, and your beliefs create your actions and your reality. If you believe that anything is possible, you will be much more likely to keep getting back up when you're knocked down, even when the path is fraught with challenges. If you believe that you alone have the capacity to take what is in your imagination and bring it to life, then you will be much more likely to make that happen! If you believe that you can turn any NO into a YES, then you will act accordingly to do so! And if you believe you can do what everyone says you can't, then you will surmount the obstacles necessary to do so and succeed!

It turns out that you have complete control over the attitude you adopt. You can choose to make lemonade out of lemons or lemons out of lemonade. As Viktor Frankl says in *Man's Search for Meaning*, "No one can take from us the ability to choose our attitudes toward the circumstances in which we find ourselves. This is the last of human freedoms."[10] Your attitude alone can make all the difference in the success of your venture and your fulfillment in life.

Lastly, even my best-reviewed products on Amazon receive some one-star reviews. There will always be people who don't like what you create, and focusing on their criticism will stall your progress. In fact, dwelling on those negative reviews would paralyze me to the extent that I would never again make another product. Truly, I would become so consumed by others' opinions that I would have no energy left to create.

Many entrepreneurs I mentor struggle with the same insecurity. They frequently share that they can't trust themselves because they're constantly seeking validation and following others' advice instead of trusting their instincts. Without an internal compass, we're prone to letting others dictate our actions rather than allowing our own heart, instinct, and moral compass to guide our decisions. Learning to trust your intuition and follow your heart takes practice. Each time you do, you strengthen your ability to make confident and independent decisions, paving the way for authentic growth and success.

Having a champion and cheerleader is crucial along your entrepreneurial journey. They provide essential emotional support and often serve as role models for cultivating a positive outlook. For me, Doug has been that person. Observing him handle seemingly insurmountable challenges with humor and resilience has inspired me to do the same. Additionally, witnessing his cup-half-full optimistic perspective over the years has bolstered my self-belief and helped transform my negative mindset to one filled with optimism.

WHAT IF I CANNOT FIND ANY INGREDIENTS THAT FASCINATE ME OR AN AOI THAT MOVES ME?

Not yet discovering an AOI might simply indicate that you haven't had enough life experiences to uncover what truly excites you. In this case, it's important to keep seeking out new experiences until you have that crystallizing experience—your defining moment of clarity. Although this process could take years, it's a fundamental part of fully embracing and enjoying life. However, not finding your AOI may also be based on a lack of mindfulness and self-awareness. If you're not fully present and engaged during your activities, you will miss out on the subtle joys or insights they offer and impede yourself from understanding which activities genuinely resonate with your core interests and thrill or fulfill you.

Mindfulness involves paying *full* attention to the present moment, and without becoming fully immersed in *this very moment*, you might overlook how an activity makes you feel. Or perhaps you're not engaging deeply enough or putting enough effort into your daily activities. If this is the case, you won't have the opportunity to fully appreciate or explore activities unless you engage deeply and give maximum effort. True engagement requires wholly immersing yourself and allowing the activity to reveal its full potential. For example, being preoccupied with external worries or distractions may prevent you from experiencing the activity's true potential to spark something deep in your heart.

Finally, your attitude toward trying new activities can dramatically impact your experience. If you approach new experiences with a cup-half-empty attitude and a sense of distrust, uncertainty, or certain fixed beliefs or mindsets, either you may not give yourself enough time to wholeheartedly explore and experience it or you'll be less open to it revealing what truly moves you. So try to approach everything with that beginner's mind and a sense of awe and wonder about what your activities might reveal. You never know what extraordinary recipe you'll create from those myriad ingredients!

As we put the final flourish on your journey through the entrepreneurial kitchen, I hope you feel better equipped to handle its heat.

The questions we've explored are not simply challenges but are aimed at helping you refine your recipe for success by providing the essential ingredients of adaptability, resilience, and a willingness to learn. Success isn't about avoiding the fire; rather, it's about learning to work in and with it, using each burn and scorch mark to add flavor to your recipe and courage to your heart. Enduring the heat is crucial to creating something extraordinary, and the most exceptional recipes are forged in the hottest fires. So keep following your curiosity, gathering your ingredients, exploring your AOI, and stirring your pot. The world is waiting for your inimitable recipe, and only you are equipped to bring it into existence.

I am here to support your entrepreneurial journey. If you have a question that I didn't address or if there's a different topic you'd like to discuss, please don't hesitate to reach out to me at Melissa @ToyingAround.com. I look forward to meeting you!

DESSERT

The Icing on the Cake

You've now served your yummy recipe to those ravenous diners. So what's next? Are your recipe-making days behind you? Well, that's entirely dependent on what step you choose to take next. Within you, there are countless new recipes waiting to be discovered, and the intoxicating part of entrepreneurship is knowing that your creativity can continue to fuel additional groundbreaking, bold ideas. The heart of entrepreneurship lies in diving inward, tapping into your innate drive, and harnessing your authentic passion, patience, and purpose to craft that unmistakable recipe from scratch. While many entrepreneurs face difficulties in replicating success after their initial triumph, the key is to keep embracing the journey of reinvention with enthusiasm instead of fear.

Rather than becoming paralyzed by continual pressure to perform, you have an amazing opportunity to continue learning, growing, and evolving once you've launched your first successful recipe. The options for how you may proceed from there are spread out like a delectable buffet, with each dish bursting with potential and the ability to bring fresh energy and innovation to your venture.

One option is to continue serving your original invention exactly as it exists, perhaps trying a few alternative marketing methods to get it out into the world but keeping its original recipe the very same. While this approach allows you to focus on maximizing the impact of your initial success, the true heart of entrepreneurship lies in continual growth, so you may want to consider how to keep your ideas fresh and competitive. If you don't go back into the pantry for new ingredients or gather new ingredients to improve and refine your current offerings, others may start replicating your brilliant idea, causing you to gradually lose your competitive edge in the market. Staying ahead of the competition requires continual reinvention.

The second option is to continue iterating and honing your original recipe. Many inventors choose to dedicate their lives to perfecting one recipe, continually tweaking and improving it. They keep that original "soup stock" and continue adding new insights and ingredients from life experience to that base rather than starting from scratch with a fresh pot and entirely novel ingredients from the pantry of life. This commitment to improvement ensures that the original recipe will become "new and improved" many times over and stay ahead of the competition. By nurturing this mindset, you will not only grow your business but continue to discover new ways to expand your original vision.

With the final option, you still keep your original recipe simmering, continuing to iterate upon it, while simultaneously placing additional pots on other burners and cooking up new ideas. This approach enables you to keep your initial recipe fresh while building a recipe pipeline. This helps maintain a continuous flow of innovative ideas, ensuring that your business stays vital, dynamic, and full of potential. Each new recipe is an opportunity for growth and a chance for you to build a continuous prep station that ensures that you never face a creative drought.

We are all capable of sustained creative success and continuous improvement. However, doing so requires an ongoing commitment to remaining open to intrigue and following this process. It's important to understand that while some attempts may not yield groundbreaking results, each step contributes additional ingredients that support your evolution and path to success.

Starting from scratch may seem daunting at times, but each time you do it, you will become more accustomed to that fear, gaining confidence in your ability to thrive in uncertainty and create something extraordinary. If you approach each day with that Start-from-Scratch mentality, even your well-established recipes will constantly evolve and advance. In fact, no concept is ever truly finished and perfected to the point where it can't be further enhanced and refined. Even a product I may have thought was nearly perfect when created often takes on a completely novel form when seen with fresh eyes down the road. The process of creating original recipes is iterative and ongoing. It continues indefinitely until you choose to write them on the menu in permanent ink and close yourself off to further exploration, discovery, and curiosity about the world around you.

With time to put those original ingredients back into a simmering pot and combine them with newly gathered, enriching life experiences, refined intuition, new insights, and fresh perspectives, your original recipe will naturally keep transforming and acquiring greater depth. In fact, other forms and iterations of that recipe will organically emerge with time. Armed with this mentality, nothing you create will ever be entirely "finished"; it will always be evolving and improving.

I experienced this iterative process over and over at M&D. I created a line of wooden magnetic dress-up figures that became a successful $10 million-a-year category for over a decade, with millions of units sold. But numerous competitors replicated our designs, and before we knew it, we had lost our market share. Worst of all, retailers complained that our products looked exactly like the copycats. I was livid at such comments, lashing out, "Wait a second; we're the inventor, and *they copied us*!" But our retailers didn't care; they just knew we had lost our innovative edge.

I was terrified that I'd be unable to improve upon our classic, but I knew that without swift reinvention, we would soon lose the category entirely to competitors. Even though we had a classic on our hands and didn't need to completely start from scratch, we still needed to infuse it with fresh pizzazz to reestablish ourselves as leaders. Therefore, I took a deep breath and threw all the existing ingredients back into the pot. Along with those ingredients, I added every bit of knowledge I had gained over that decade about what customers loved most about the magnetic dress-ups, what they loved about our products more generally, and what sold best, along with a dash of current insights and trends. I let all those ingredients simmer together, and after about one week, something miraculous emerged! It was a reinvigorated, even better version of our original magnetic dress-up that reestablished our leadership in the category.

By adopting a Start-from-Scratch mentality, which is crucial for being a lifelong creative entrepreneur, you'll find that it becomes second nature. As you grow more comfortable with the process, continuing to stock your pantry with diverse ingredients and learning to trust your intuition, this approach will evolve and become even more refined to better serve both you and your customers. Over time, developing innovative recipes and presenting them to eager consumers will become your heart of entrepreneurship and the icing on your cake!

I would love to hear your thoughts on the recipe process detailed on these pages. As a fellow lifelong learner and practitioner of these practices, I genuinely welcome all feedback, whether it's praise, criticism, or a mix of both. Your insights will help me refine, balance, and enhance the recipe, allowing it to evolve and become better suited to serve you! And that's the beauty of the creative process!

RESOURCES

I have been fascinated with the topic of creativity for decades and have read hundreds of relevant books and articles. My personal metaphor of our brains as a commercial kitchen emerged both from that research and from studying my own creative process for over a half-century. Having read so many books and articles simply for enjoyment and never knowing I would write a book on the topic, I didn't take meticulous notes—and in some cases, I don't necessarily even know where their thoughts ended and my own began. I have done my best to comb through my sources and properly acknowledge the derivation of my ideas, but in the event that I have missed anything, I am listing the books and articles that discuss the stages of creativity outside those listed in the endnotes. Thank you to all the incredible, brilliant researchers and creatives who helped me understand how creativity works and provided the inspiration for how to create my own unique recipe for success.

Csikszentmihalyi, Mihaly & Sawyer, Keith, "Creative Insight: The Social Dimension of a Solitary Movement," in *The Nature of Insight*, eds. R. J. Sternberg and J. E. Davidson (MIT Press, 1995).

Csikszentmihalyi, Mihaly, *Creativity: Flow and the Psychology of Discovery and Invention* (HarperCollins, 1996).

Ghiselin, Brewster, ed, *The Creative Process: Reflections on Invention in the Arts and Sciences* (University of California Press, 1954).

Hadamard, Jacques, *Descriptions of Illumination: An Essay on the Psychology of the Invention in the Mathematical Field* (Princeton University Press, 1949).

Simonton, Dean Keith, *Origins of Genius: Darwinian Perspectives on Creativity* (Oxford University Press, 1999).

Wallas, Graham, *The Art of Thought* (Harcourt, Brace and Company, 1926).

NOTES

INTRODUCTION
1. "Anxiety in a Troubled World: Panel Discussion and Q&A Session," May 9, 2024, organized by Onlinevents.co.uk.
2. Personal Zoom conversation with the author, June 24, 2024.
3. Tal Ben-Shahar, *Learn the Secrets to Daily Joy and Lasting Fulfillment* (McGraw Hill, 2007), 25.
4. A. C. Shilton, "You Accomplished Something Great. So Now What?," *New York Times*, May 28, 2019.
5. "The Founder Resilience Research 2024: Fueling Founder Resilience" (Foundology, 2024), 12–13. Supported by Entrerprise Educators, Imperial Enterprise Lab and UCL School of Management.

CHAPTER 1: THE MINDSET OF AUTHENTIC ENTREPRENEURS
1. Shunryū Suzuki, *Zen Mind, Beginner's Mind*, ed. Trudy Dixon (Weatherhill, 1970), 21.
2. Matthijs Baas, Barbara Nevicka, and Femke S. Ten Velden, "Specific Mindfulness Skills Differentially Predict Creative Performance," *Personality and Social Psychology Bulletin* 40, no. 3 (2014).
3. Rachel Adcock, Duke Associate Professor of Psychiatry and Behavioral Sciences, talk at Innovation & Entrepreneurship Advisory Board Meeting, April 12, 2024.

4. Mihaly Csikszentmihalyi, *Flow—The Psychology of Optimal Experience* (HarperCollins Perennial, 1990), ch. 3.

CHAPTER 2: GATHER YOUR INGREDIENTS

1. Dictionary.com, s.v.: "Intrigue," accessed September 8, 2024, dictionary.com/browse/intrigue.
2. Dictionary.com, s.v.: "Indiscriminate," accessed September 14, 2024, dictionary.com/browse/indiscriminate.
3. Intrinsic motivation concept explained in Teresa Amabile, "Motivation and Creativity: Effects of Motivational Orientation on Creative Writers," *Journal of Personality and Social Psychology* (American Psychological Association 1985), 393–399.
4. Merriam-Webster.com, s.v.: "Autotelic," accessed September 18, 2024, merriam-webster.com/dictionary/autotelic.
5. Joseph Walters and Howard Gardner, *The Crystallizing Experience: Discovering an Intellectual Gift* (Harvard Project Zero, 1984), 4–7.
6. Walters and Gardner, *The Crystallizing Experience*, 6.
7. Dean Keith Simonton, *Origins of Genius: Darwinian Perspectives on Creativity* (Oxford University Press, 1999), 85.
8. Amanda Athuraliya, "Divergent vs. Convergent Thinking: What's the Difference?," Creately.com, October 12, 2023, creately.com/guides/divergent-vs-convergent-thinking/.
9. Janet E. Davidson and Robert J. Sternberg, eds., *The Psychology of Problem Solving* (Cambridge University Press, 2003).
10. I have read numerous articles and books on intuition, including Kenneth S. Bowers, Glenn Regehr, Claude Balthazard, and Kevin Parker, "Intuition in the Context of Discovery," *Cognitive Psychology* 22 (1990), 72–110; R. M. Hogarth, *Educating Intuition* (University of Chicago Press, 2001), 70–75, 207, 214, 251–253; Simon M. McCrae, "Intuition, Insight, and the Right Hemisphere: Emergence of Higher Sociocognitive Functions," *Psychology Research Behavioral Management* 3 (2010), 1–39, doi: 10.2147/prbm.s7935.

11. Mihaly Csikszentmihalyi, *Creativity: Flow and the Psychology of Discovery and Invention* (HarperCollins, 1996), 116.
12. Mihaly Csikszentmihalyi, *Flow—The Psychology of Optimal Experience* (HarperCollins Perennial, 1990), 71.
13. Csikszentmihalyi, 40.
14. Mihaly Csikszentmihalyi, *The Evolving Self: A Psychology for the Third Millennium* (HarperCollins, 1993).
15. "Story of Velcro," Lemelson Center, Smithsonian Institute, April 15, 2014, invention.si.edu/invention-stories/george-de-mestral-velcror-inventor.
16. "Story of the Microwave Oven," Whirlpool Corporation, whirlpool.com/blog/kitchen/history-of-microwave.html.

CHAPTER 3: ALLOW YOUR INGREDIENTS TO SIMMER

1. Mihaly Csikszentmihalyi, *Creativity: Flow and the Psychology of Discovery and Invention* (HarperCollins, 1996), 102.
2. Stratfordchef.com, "10 Steps of Stock Production SCS Open Kitchen," Chef Eli Silverhorne, stratfordchef.com/wp-content/uploads/2020/04/Stocks_OpenKitchen_EliSilverthorne.pdf.
3. Merriam-Webster.com, s.v.: "Scum," accessed September 25, 2024, merriam-webster.com/dictionary/scum.
4. Nancy Andreasen, *The Creative Brain: The Science of Genius* (Penguin Group, 2005); Graham Wallas, *The Art of Thought* (Harcourt, Brace and Company, 1926).
5. Brewster Ghiselin, ed., *The Creative Process: Reflections on Invention in the Arts and Sciences* (University of California Press, 1985).
6. Rosamund E. M. Harding, *An Anatomy of Inspiration and an Essay on the Creative Mood* (Litt. D. W. Hefner & Sons Ltd., 1949), 104–105.
7. Andreasen, *The Creative Brain*, 42.
8. General list taken from Ghiselin, *The Creative Process*.

9. Dan Pilat and Dr. Sekoul Krastev, "Why Do We Favor Our Existing Beliefs?," The Decision Lab, thedecisionlab.com/biases/confirmation-bias.
10. Gustave LeBon, *The Crowd: A Study of the Popular Mind*, 2nd ed. (Macmillan, 1895), ch. 2.
11. William Trotter, *The Attack-Escape Reaction* (Macmillan, 1908).
12. Alan Walsh, "Space Education & Strategic Applications," *Space Education & Strategic Applications* 1, no. 1, 4.

CHAPTER 4: YOUR RECIPE IS READY

1. Kenneth S. Bowers, Glenn Regehr, Claude Balthazard, and Kevin Parker, "Intuition in the Context of Discovery," *Cognitive Psychology* 22 (1990), 72–110; R. M. Hogarth, *Educating Intuition* (University of Chicago Press, 2001), 70–75, 207, 214, 251–253; Simon M. McCrae, "Intuition, Insight, and the Right Hemisphere: Emergence of Higher Sociocognitive Functions," *Psychology Research Behavioral Management* 3 (2010), 1–39, doi: 10.2147/prbm.s7935.
2. K. Anders Ericsson, Robert R. Hoffman, Aaron Kozbelt, and A. Mark Williams, eds., *The Cambridge Handbook of Expertise and Expert Performance* (Cambridge University Press, 2018).
3. Jennifer A. Williams, *Heartmanity* Blog, September 2025, blog.heartmanity.com/author/jennifer-a-williams-emotional-intelligence-coach.
4. Jerry Mayer and John P. Holms, eds., *Bite-Size Einstein: Quotations on Just About Everything from the Greatest Mind of the Twentieth Century* (Gramercy Books, 1996), 17.
5. Søren Kierkegaard, *The Concept of Anxiety*, trans. Alastair Hannay (Liverlight, 2014), 188.

CHAPTER 5: ASSESS AND ALTER YOUR RECIPE

1. Mark Twain, *Mark Twain's Own Autobiography: The Chapters from the North American Review*, ed. Michael J. Kiskis (University of Wisconsin Press, 1990), 185.

2. Isaac Newton, letter to Robert Hooke, February 5, 1675/6, in *The Correspondence of Isaac Newton*, vol. 1, ed. H. W. Turnbull (Cambridge University Press, 1959), 416.

CHAPTER 6: PRESENT YOUR RECIPE
1. Noam Wasserman, *The Founder's Dilemmas* (Princeton University Press, 2013), 3.
2. Brian Sutter, "The #1 Reason Small Businesses Fail—and How to Avoid It," *Score Foundation*, June 1, 2019, score.org/resource/blog-post/1-reason-small-businesses-fail-and-how-avoid-it.

CHAPTER 7: FOOD FOR THOUGHT
1. Albert Szent-Gyorgy, *The Scientist Speculates: An Anthology of Partly-Baked Ideas*, ed. I. J. Good (Heinemann, 1962), 14.
2. Carol S. Dweck, *Mindset: The New Psychology of Success* (Ballantine Books, 2006).
3. Dale Carnegie, *How to Stop Worrying and Start Living* (Pocket Books, 1948), 58.
4. Dean Keith Simonton, *Origins of Genius: Darwinian Perspectives on Creativity* (Oxford University Press, 1999), 155. Actual quote is "the creators with the most masterpieces will be those with the most ignored and neglected products."
5. Simonton, *Origins of Genius*, 163–165.
6. James Clear, *Atomic Habits: An Easy & Proven Way to Build Good Habits & Break Bad Ones* (Avery, 2018), 22.
7. Simonton, *Origins of Genius*, 163–165.
8. Patrick Vlaskovits, "Henry Ford, Innovation, and That 'Faster Horse' Quote," *Harvard Business Review*, August 29, 2011, hbr.org/2011/08/henry-ford-never-said-the-fast.
9. Rachel Adcock, Duke Associate Professor of Psychiatry and Behavioral Sciences, talk at Innovation & Entrepreneurship Advisory Board Meeting, April 12, 2024.
10. Viktor E. Frankl, *Man's Search for Meaning* (Beacon Press, 2006), 86.

ABOUT THE AUTHOR

Melissa Bernstein is an entrepreneur, creative, and mother of six. She's cofounder of the billion-dollar toy company Melissa & Doug and cofounder of Lifelines, a wellness brand offering science-backed sensory immersion products designed to help manage stress, find calm, and enhance well-being. Melissa is the entrepreneur in residence for the Inner MBA certification program created by Sounds True, LinkedIn, and Wisdom 2.0; cofounder of Duke University's Melissa & Doug Entrepreneurs program; Duke University Trustee; and author of *Lifelines* and *Practice Makes Purpose*.

ABOUT SOUNDS TRUE

Sounds True was founded in 1985 by Tami Simon with a clear mission: to disseminate spiritual wisdom. Since starting out as a project with one woman and her tape recorder, we have grown into a multimedia publishing company with a catalog of more than 3,000 titles by some of the leading teachers and visionaries of our time, and an ever-expanding family of beloved customers from across the world.

In more than three decades of evolution, Sounds True has maintained our focus on our overriding purpose and mission: to wake up the world. We offer books, audio programs, online learning experiences, and in-person events to support your personal growth and awakening, and to unlock our greatest human capacities to love and serve.

At SoundsTrue.com you'll find a wealth of resources to enrich your journey, including our weekly *Insights at the Edge* podcast, free downloads, and information about our nonprofit Sounds True Foundation, where we strive to remove financial barriers to the materials we publish through scholarships and donations worldwide.

To learn more, please visit SoundsTrue.com/freegifts or call us toll-free at 800.333.9185.

Together, we can wake up the world.